The Protevangelium of James

TOOLS AND TRANSLATIONS

The Westar Tools and Translations series provides critical tools and fresh new translations for research on canonical and non-canonical texts that survive from the earliest periods of the Christian tradition to the Middle Ages. These writings are crucial for determining the complex history of Christian origins. The translations are known as the Scholars Version. Each work, whether a translation or research aid, is accompanied by textual notes, translation notes, cross references, and an index. An extensive introduction also sets out the challenge a text or research aid addresses.

EARLY CHRISTIAN APOCRYPHA

Editorial Board:
TONY BURKE
BRENT LANDAU
JANET SPITTLER

Translations of non-canonical texts out of the Christian tradition are offered as part of the Westar Tools and Translations series in cooperation with the North American Society for the Study of Christian Apocrypha (NASSCAL). The Early Christian Apocrypha series features fresh new translations of major apocryphal texts that survive from the early period of the Christian church. These non-canonical writings are crucial for determining the complex history of Christian origins. The series continues the work of Julian V. Hills, who edited the first six volumes of the series for Polebridge Press.

Volume 1: *The Acts of Andrew*
Volume 2: *The Epistle of the Apostles*
Volume 3: *The Acts of Thomas*
Volume 4: *The Acts of Peter*
Volume 5: *Didache*
Volume 6: *The Acts of John*
Volume 7: *The Protevangelium of James*
Volume 8: *The Gospel of Pseudo-Matthew and the Nativity of Mary*

The Protevangelium of James

Lily C. Vuong

CASCADE *Books* · Eugene, Oregon

THE PROTEVANGELIUM OF JAMES
Early Christian Apocrypha 7

Cascade Books
An Imprint of Wipf and Stock Publishers
199 W. 8th Ave., Suite 3
Eugene, OR 97401

www.wipfandstock.com

PAPERBACK ISBN: 978-1-5326-5617-0
HARDCOVER ISBN: 978-1-5326-5618-7
EBOOK ISBN: 978-1-5326-5619-4

Cataloguing-in-Publication data:

Names: Vuong, Lily C., 1978–, author

Title: The Protevangelium of James / Lily C. Vuong.

Description: Eugene, OR: Cascade Books, 2018. | Early Christian Apocrypha 7. |
   Includes bibliographical references and index.

Identifiers: ISBN: 978-1-5326-5617-0 (paperback). | ISBN: 978-1-5326-5618-7
   (hardcover). | ISBN: 978-1-5326-5619-4 (ebook).

Subjects: LCSH: Protevanglium Jacobi—Criticism, interpretation, etc.

Classification: BS2860.3 V8661 2019 (print). | BS2860.3 (epub).

Manufactured in the U.S.A.   06/05/19

For Olivia Grace and Gabriel James

Contents

Acknowledgments

WHEN I WAS FIRST approached to write a new translation and commentary for the *Protevangelium of James*, I was excited at the prospect of diving back into this rich and entertaining apocryphal narrative on the early life of the Virgin Mary after having spent a good deal of time writing and publishing my dissertation on the topic. It was perhaps serendipitous that I was working on another project for a book series at the time whose main editor was Ronald Hock. After informing him that I would be writing this new commentary with the same book series he wrote his commentary on the *Protevangelium of James* twenty-three years earlier, he immediately and very generously mailed me everything he thought I'd find useful – articles, rare books, and even his own handwritten notes on the topic. I am incredibly grateful for being the recipient of such invaluable resources and am thankful to Ron for his kindness and support.

This new translation would not have been possible without the invitation from the series editors of the Early Christian Apocrypha Series and the North American Society for the Study of Christian Apocryphal Literature (NASSCAL), especially Tony Burke who read every draft and offered critical and helpful notes and comments, significantly improving its content and style and preventing any missteps; I am wholly indebted to his careful attention to detail. I am also thankful to Brent Landau, Janet Spittler, and Eric Vanden Eykel who read and provided thoughtful and useful comments during the final stages of the manuscript.

Given that my interest in the *Protevangelium* can be traced all the way back to my studies in graduate school, I am thankful to Annette Yoshiko Reed, Stephen Shoemaker, Tobias Nicklas, and Pierluigi Piovanelli, who played key roles in informing and refining my thinking of Apocryphal literature.

I would also like to thank my colleagues at Central Washington University and to the School of Graduate Studies and Research for their support for this project. Additionally, I owe many thanks to Kevin McGinnis for his helpful notes on my translation, Olivia Bode, who aided me with many copy-editing issues, and the editorial staff at Wipf and Stock, especially Matthew Wimer, K. C. Hanson, and Ian Creeger, for guiding the book through publication.

As always, I owe my greatest debt to my family. Special thanks go to Eileen Jankowski who read and edited the manuscript several times, and who has always been a great source of support and encouragement. To my children, Olivia and Gabriel, for making my life richer and more exciting, but also for understanding all the extra hours I had to spend at the office. Above all, I am grateful to my husband, James, for his unwavering love and support and for taking on more than his share of the parenting responsibilities while I worked to bring this project to completion.

Lily C. Vuong
Central Washington University
Ellensburg, Washington
August 2018

Abbreviations and Conventions

Ancient

Ascen. Isa.	*Ascension of Isaiah*
b. San.	*Babylonian Talmud Sanhedrin*
1 Clem.	*1 Clement*

Clement of Alexandria

Strom.	*Stromateis*
3 Cor.	*3 Corinthians*

Hippolytus

Trad. Ap.	*Traditio apostolica*
Hist. Jos. Carp.	*History of Joseph the Carpenter*

Ignatius

Eph.	*Epistle to the Ephesians*
Inf. Gos. Thom.	*Infancy Gospel of Thomas*

Irenaeus

Epid.	*Epideixis tou apostolikou kērygmatos*
Haer.	*Adversus haereses*

Jerome

Helv.	*Adversus Helvidium de Mariae virginitate perpetua*
Jos. Asen.	*Joseph and Aseneth*

Josephus

    A.J.   *Antiquitates judaicae*

    B.J.   *Bellum judaicum*

Justin Martyr

    1 Apol.   *First Apology*

    Dial.   *Dialogue with Trypho*

LAB   *Liber antiquitatum biblicarum*

LAE   *Life of Adam and Eve*

m. Ket.   *Mishnah Ketubbot*

m. Nid.   *Mishnah Niddah*

m. Sotah   *Mishnah Sotah*

m. Ta'an.   *Mishnah Ta'anit*

m. Yoma   *Mishnah Yoma*

Nat. Mary   *Nativity of Mary*

Origen

    Cels.   *Contra Celsum*

    Comm. Matt. *Commentarium in evangelium Matthaei*

    Hom. Luc.   *Homiliae in Lucam*

Philo

    Mos.   *De vita Mosis*

    Somn.   *De Somniis*

    Spec.   *De specialibus legibus*

Prot. Jas.   *Protevangelium of James*

Ps.-Mt.   *Gospel of Pseudo-Matthew*

Rev. Magi   *Revelation of the Magi*

T. Adam   *Testament of Adam*

T. Benj.   *Testament of Benjamin*

T. Dan   *Testament of Dan*

T. Gad	*Testament of Gad*
T. Levi	*Testament of Levi*
t. Hull.	*Tosefta Hullin*
t. Pesah.	*Tosefta Pesahim*

Tertullian

Carn. Chr.	*De carne Christi*
Virg.	*De virginibus velandis*

Modern

ANRW	*Aufstieg und Niedergang der römischen Welt*
CCSA	Corpus Christianorum: Series apocryphorum
CRRAI	Compte rendu, Rencontre Assyriologique Internationale
CSCO	Corpus Scriptorum Christianorum Orientalium
CSEL	Corpus Scriptorum Ecclesiasticorum Latinorum
ExpT	*Expository Times*
GCS	Die griechische christliche Schriftsteller der ersten [drei] Jahrhunderte
HTR	*Harvard Theological Review*
JECS	*Journal of Early Christian Studies*
JJS	*Journal of Jewish Studies*
JQR	*Jewish Quarterly Review*
LCL	Loeb Classical Library
NTTS	New Testament Tools and Studies
NovT	*Novum Testamentum*
PG	Patrologia Graeca
SBFA	Studium Biblicum Franciscanum Analecta
SBLSP	Society of Biblical Literature Seminar Papers
SH	Subsidia Hagiographica
TS	*Theological Studies*

TSK	*Theologische Studien und Kritiken*
TUGAL	Texte und Untersuchungen zur Geschichte der altchristlichen Literatur
VT	*Vetus Testamentum*
WUNT	Wissenschaftliche Untersuchungen zum Neuen Testament

Conventions

HB	Hebrew Bible
LXX	Septuagint
NT	New Testament

Introduction

ON DISPLAY AT THE Yale University Art Gallery is a painting from Dura-Europos, an ancient city in eastern Syria and the location of major excavations in the 1920s and 1930s. Yale archaeologists found the painting in the remains of a third-century house that was used as a church—the earliest Christian church ever discovered. On the southern wall of the building's baptistery is the image of a woman drawing water from a well, while looking over her left shoulder. While most scholars have assumed it is a depiction of the Samaritan woman narrated from the Gospel of John, Michael Peppard has suggested that the painting is better interpreted as Mary at the well.[1] The canonical Gospels of Matthew and Luke do not give a specific location for the Annunciation, despite general assumptions that place the scene at her home based on centuries-long depictions of the Annunciation in Western art. While the scene of Mary drawing water from the well or spring is not a detail found in the canonical infancy narratives, it is a feature of the *Protevangelium of James* (*Protevangelium* hereafter) in which the divine voice attempts to make contact with Mary to announce her special role in salvation history (*Prot. Jas.* 11:1–9). Additionally, the image also depicts a vacant space behind the woman, most likely representing the invisible divine voice of the Annunciation,[2] a detail again found in the *Protevangelium* which describes a bodiless voice speaking to Mary before the appearance of an angel; hence Mary is said to have been looking "all around her, to the right and left, to see from where the voice was coming" (*Prot. Jas.* 11:3). If Peppard's

1. Peppard, *World's Oldest Church*, 155–201.

2. There are two possible options for the identity of the voice: the angel Gabriel, who appears after Mary retreats to her house or the divine voice of God. In Rabbinic literature, *bat kol*, "daughter of a voice" is commonly interpreted as the voice or presence of God. See Zervos, "Early Non-Canonical Annunciation," 682–86.

1

interpretation is correct, this painting would be the oldest depiction of Mary's Annunciation at the well. This interpretation is especially intriguing given that in the same house church a procession of women walking towards a large building with doors is also depicted. On the east wall, the feet and bottom garments of five women approach the structure. On the west wall three full women are each carrying a lit candle.[3] Admittedly, there is no consensus on the identities of the women in the image, but Gertrud Schiller is convinced that the women are the virgins who guide Mary to the temple (*Prot. Jas.* 7:4).[4] If these two proposals are correct, then the church house at Dura-Europos would appear to display artistically two dominant themes informed by this apocryphal text.

While the *Protevangelium*'s presence and impact on the Dura-Europos church house is debatable, there is no doubt regarding the *Protevangelium*'s influence on early Christian traditions, practices, and forms of piety associated with the Virgin Mary. Offering rich details from Mary's miraculous conception by her mother Anna to her own conception and birth of Jesus, this narrative stands as the foundation for her prevailing depiction as extraordinarily pure and holy, but also for later apocryphal, hagiographical, and liturgical writings. Despite its early date, this document's contributions to Marian piety and devotion cannot be overestimated.[5] Surviving in at least 140 Greek manuscripts and translated into multiple languages including Syriac, Georgian, Latin, Armenian, Arabic, Coptic, Ethiopic, and Slavonic (see section on transmission below), the *Protevangelium*'s frequent copying attests to its popularity throughout the Christian world.[6] Moreover, the text functions as a source for a vari-

3. Peppard, *World's Oldest Church*, 111–54.

4. Cf. in *Ps.-Mt.* 10 and *Nat. Mary* 7, 8; Schiller, *Ikonographie der christlichen Kunst*, vol. 3, fig. 1. Dinker ("Die ersten Petrusdarstellungen," 12) believes that the women carrying candles are the five wise virgins from Matthew 25; A. Grabar (*Early Christian Art*, 68–71, fig. 59) has identified the figures as the women who approach Jesus' tomb. At the Exodus chapel in Egypt, however, there is an image labeled *parthenoi* depicting the temple virgins' procession. Its date ranges between the fifth and seventh centuries (images and discussion in Cartlidge and Elliott, *Art and the Christian Apocrypha*, 36–37).

5. There are no specific prayers or cult in honor of Mary in the *Protevangelium*, but its foundations for Marian piety with its elaborate and expanded descriptions of Mary's life is undeniable. For the influence of the *Protevangelium* on Marian piety and devotion, see esp. Shoemaker, *Mary in Early Christian Faith and Devotion*, 47–61 (on devotion) and 53–54 (on piety).

6. See de Strycker, "Handschriften," 588–607; Daniels, "Greek Manuscript Tradition"; and Zervos, "Prolegomena," on the Greek manuscript tradition. See Elliott,

ety of later writings on the life of Mary, including the *Gospel of Pseudo-Matthew*, the *Nativity of Mary*, the *Armenian* and *Arabic Gospels of the Infancy*, the *History of Joseph the Carpenter*, and Maximus the Confessor's *Life of the Virgin.*[7] From its use in liturgical readings for various feasts, including Mary's Nativity, Conception, and Presentation, to its inspiration for numerous artistic representations found in church paintings, mosaics, and sarcophagi, the text enjoyed near canonical status despite its categorization as apocryphal.

As a narrative that features characters and events from the NT text but lacks a presence in the canon, the *Protevangelium* fits the criteria for extracanonical and apocryphal literature. However, other features attributed to works deemed apocryphal, including its rejection as a possible candidate into the NT canon, seem problematic not least because of its popularity and influence on early Christian practices, traditions, and beliefs. In his study of this categorization process, François Bovon proposed that church leaders, theologians, and ordinary Christians did not simply distinguish between canonical and apocryphal texts or accepted and rejected texts; rather, they were familiar with a third category of writing which were, according to Bovon, "useful for the soul."[8] Such writings functioned as the basis for religious life in the early church and were deeply cherished by the masses and even sometimes relied upon by orthodox leadership.[9] Stephen Shoemaker has argued that Marian apocrypha is better understood not as failed scripture but as an accepted part of ecclesiastical tradition,[10] and that the *Protevangelium* in particular should be more appropriately understood as "quasi-canonical" given its vast influence on Christian tradition.[11]

Apocryphal New Testament, 52–57, for a list of the most important ancient and modern translations and manuscripts and de Santos Otero (*Die handschriftliche Überlieferung*, 2:1–32) who has also catalogued 169 Slavonic manuscripts of the *Protevangelium* and related texts.

7. Special consideration for the way these works have used and deviated from the *Protevangelium* will be addressed in the present volume.

8. Bovon, "Beyond the Canonical and Apocryphal Books," 125–37; and Bovon, "Useful for the Soul," 185–95.

9. Epiphanius of Salamis (d. 403), for instance, cites apocryphal material as an authoritative part of Christian tradition when he recounts information about Mary's parents that is most definitely drawn from the *Protevangelium*.

10. Shoemaker, "Between Scripture and Tradition," 492.

11. Shoemaker, *Mary in Early Christian Faith and Devotion*, 49.

As a highly influential text about the most prominent woman in Christian history, the *Protevangelium*'s traditions were widely disseminated in later popular literature such as the *Gospel of Pseudo-Matthew* and its derivative, the *Nativity of Mary*, each of which are witnessed in at least a hundred manuscripts. Instead of being perceived as a rejected scripture, it was received with some authority for helping understand questions about how Mary was conceived, what she was like as a child, and why she was chosen to give birth to the son of God; in addition, the text provides understanding of her role in salvation history and how and why she should be venerated.

Summary

Since Mary stands as the unequivocal center of the *Protevangelium*, the narrative's contents are marked by the various stages in her life and are shaped by a deep desire to understand her for her own sake, particularly why and how she came to be praised for holding the paradoxical role of Virgin Mother. The text is dependent upon and clearly reworks elements of the canonical gospels of Matthew and Luke, but Jesus' nativity scene, which commences during the last quarter of the narrative, comprises only a fraction of the text. The narrative focuses squarely and deliberately on Mary's character and her role and contributions to Christian history. The following summary serves not only to describe the basic plot of the narrative, but also to point out several comparisons to its canonical sources as well as to other literary influences on the text.

Mary's Pre-Story and Conception

The *Protevangelium* opens with information about Mary's parents, Joachim and Anna, the circumstances of Mary's birth, as well as the community in which they lived—precisely the information lacking in the Gospels of Matthew and Luke. Reminiscent of great biblical couples (e.g., Sarah and Abraham; Elizabeth and Zechariah), we discover that despite their good standing in the community and their wealth (*Prot. Jas.* 1:1), Joachim and Anna suffer from infertility. The initial scene is set at the Jerusalem temple wherein Joachim's double offering of sacrifice is rejected because of his childlessness (1:5). After confirming in the "Book of the Twelve Tribes of Israel" that he alone stands childless, Joachim runs off into the wilderness, fasting forty days and forty nights, to lament and wait for an explanation from God for his situation (1:6–7).

Aware that childbearing is a blessing awarded to the righteous by God (Gen 3:14), Anna too responds by wailing not only because of her barren state but also because she believes she is now a widow given Joachim's disappearance (2:1). Anna's cries elicit a rebuke from her slave girl that sends Anna into the garden to offer a poignant lament over how she alone is fruitless in such a fruitful world: "because even the [birds, beasts, animals, waters, earth] reproduce before you, O Lord" (3:1–8). Anna's pain and embarrassment ceases, however, upon the arrival of an angel of the Lord who informs her that she will indeed conceive and that her child will be "spoken of throughout the whole world" (4:1). Anna immediately dedicates her child to life-long service to the Lord (4:2), confirming that her childlessness was the result of unlucky circumstances rather than a deficiency of righteousness.

Joachim also is the recipient of an angelic visit when he is informed of his wife's new status (4:4), prompting him first to gather his flocks for a sacrificial offering (4:5–7), and only secondarily to return home to celebrate with his wife (4:8). Joachim's righteousness is separately confirmed upon presenting his gifts at the temple and finding "no sin" indicated on the prophetic leafed headdress worn by the priest (5:2). Straightaway, the *Protevangelium* establishes Joachim and Anna as righteous and pious people fit to parent the child who would be the mother of the son of God.

Mary's Birth, Infancy, and Stay at the Jerusalem Temple

In due time, Anna gives birth to her miraculous child and makes clear she is honored by her daughter, whom she names Mary (5:5–8). As expected of the "miraculous child being born to a once barren mother" motif, Mary's life is immediately marked as exceptional—particularly with respect to her purity, but also by her agility and physical growth. In addition to waiting the prescribed days before nursing Mary (5:9), Anna is said to have transformed Mary's bedroom into a sanctuary so that no "profane or unclean" person or thing can make contact with her daughter; Mary's only companions are the "undefiled daughters of the Hebrews" (6:4–5). After Mary amazingly walks seven steps at the age of six months, Anna swoops her up, vowing her feet will not touch the ground again until she is taken up to the temple (6:1–5). Contact with the outside world takes place during a magnificent banquet in honor of Mary's first birthday (6:6). At the celebration, Mary is given a double blessing (first by the temple priests and second by the high priests), the first of which is followed by an "amen" from all the people, reinforcing universally the blessed status and role of Mary (6:7–9). After the banquet, Anna sings another prayer, but this time the tone is joyful, thankful, and full of hope (6:11–13). When Mary reaches the age of two, Anna and Joachim discuss their vow to send Mary to the temple, but ultimately decide to wait one more year (7:1). The year passes and then the undefiled daughters of the Hebrews are summoned to help Mary with the move from her parent's house to God's house (7:4–5). Anna's and Joachim's fear that Mary will have a difficult transition are alleviated upon seeing her dance at the altar, receiving love and blessings from the priests and the whole house of Israel (7:9–10). Mary spends her childhood at the sacred Jerusalem temple, nurtured like a dove and fed by a heavenly angel (8:2).

Mary's Adolescent Years: From Girlhood to Womanhood

After a nine-year time lapse, Mary's approaching twelfth birthday sets the scene for the second part of the narrative. However, unlike the banquet celebration of her first birthday, this anniversary is marked by the fear of the priests that Mary's transition from childhood to womanhood might "defile the temple of the Lord our God" (8:4). Concerned for both the sanctity of the temple and Mary's well-being, the priests have Zechariah, the high priest, pray for guidance (8:5). Zechariah's prayer is answered when an angel of the Lord appears and instructs him to gather all the widowers in town to determine by lot who should be chosen to guard Mary (8:7–9). Leaving Mary's fate to God, the priest pays heed to the instructions, facilitating the arrival of Joseph on the scene, who is depicted differently and more fully than the canonical Gospels—he is old and already a father of sons (9:8). Reminiscent of Num 17:1–9 where Aaron's staff buds to signal the selection of the proper priestly line, Joseph is chosen by God's will when a dove springs from his rod and then lands on his head (9:5–6). Though resistant to the selection at first, Joseph is warned of the consequences when God's intentions are disregarded and takes Mary (now described as the Virgin of the Lord) home under his guardianship (9:11–12).

The Annunciation and Mary as the Lord's Virgin

Immediately after returning home, Joseph departs to build houses, leaving Mary under the watch of the Lord alone (9:12); Mary is soon summoned back to the temple to help weave the temple curtain. Reinforcing Mary's royal lineage, the high priest remembers to include her among the other virgins found from the tribe of David to spin (10:1–6). By lot, Mary is given the scarlet and pure purple threads (10:7), symbolic of virtuousness and royalty, respectively. While working on her part of the curtain, one day Mary ventures out to a public space to draw some water (from a well or a spring)—a drastic contrast to the previous depiction of her private and enclosed childhood bedroom chambers and her stay at the temple. Only in this outdoor space is Mary first called upon by a bodiless voice that offers her greetings and blessings. Unable to locate the voice's source, Mary returns to her house frightened (11:1–4). Perhaps to distract herself, Mary returns to her spinning only to be physically approached by an angel of the Lord who tells her not to fear because she is favored by the Lord and has been chosen to "conceive from his Word" (11:5). As in the Annunciation scene in Luke, but in a more creative manner and with additional details, Mary converses with the angel over how this conception will transpire given her status as a virgin. After the angel explains that she will not give birth like other women and that the power of God will overshadow her, she is instructed to name her child Jesus because "he will save his people from their sins" (11:7).

After fully consenting to her new role, Mary presents her part of the curtain to the high priest who blesses Mary's work and says she will be "blessed among all the generations of the earth" (12:2). Mary then visits her kinswoman, Elizabeth. Miraculously expecting a child herself (the future John the Baptist), Elizabeth, much like her depiction in Luke, acknowledges Mary's present state as significant and remarkable so much so that the child inside her has sprung up to bless her (12:5). However, unlike Luke's depiction, Elizabeth does not offer praise of Mary for believing in the divine word nor does Mary respond with a song of praise (cf. the Magnificat of Luke 1:46–56). Instead, and oddly enough, Mary has actually forgotten the exchange she had with the angel Gabriel and again questions why she is the recipient of all these blessings. This exchange is not commented on further; instead, Mary is said to have simply stayed with Elizabeth for three months while her belly grew. Frightened and still unclear of how her situation came to be, the visibly pregnant Mary, now sixteen years of age, decides to return home to hide her condition from the "children of Israel" (12:6–9).

Joseph Returns Home to Mary at Six Months Pregnant

After three months have passed, Joseph returns home to find Mary six months pregnant and unable to explain her condition (cf. Matt 1:18). Breaking into a despairing lament over Mary's pregnancy and his own failure to keep her safe, Joseph evokes an Adam and Eve analogy: just as Eve was deceived and defiled while alone, the same too has happened to Mary. Assuming that Mary is guilty of adultery, Joseph's initial reaction of fright turns into an aggressive and accusatory questioning of his wife: "You who have been cared for by God —why have you done this? Have you forgotten the Lord your God? Why have you shamed your soul . . . ?" (13:6–7). After weeping bitterly, Mary responds to Joseph's questions confidently and directly: "I am pure and have not known a man [sexually]," but is still unable to explain how she is pregnant (13:8–10). Joseph's anger subsides, but he returns to a state of fear as he contemplates what he should do with her. Afraid that keeping the situation secret will get him into trouble with the law, but also that revealing it will result in an innocent death, Joseph contemplates divorcing her quietly (14:2–4; cf. Matt 1:19). Resolution comes when an angel appears to Joseph in a dream explaining to him that the child inside Mary was conceived by the Holy Spirit and that he will be responsible for "sav[ing] his people from their sins" (14:6 cf. Matt 1:20–23). After finding out the truth about Mary's situation, Joseph glorifies God and recommits to his task of guarding the Virgin of the Lord.

Mary's and Joseph's Purity Tested

When Joseph's absence at the council is noticed, Annas the scribe decides to inquire about his whereabouts only to find the temple virgin they put under his care is now pregnant (15:1–3). Joseph's role as Mary's protector or guardian is tested again. This time, however, the results are positive and Joseph stays loyal to Mary and stands trial for the accusations made by the temple priests (15:10–12, 14–15). Both Mary and Joseph are questioned harshly over the pregnancy and accused of humiliating themselves and lying—ironically, much in the same tone that Joseph used when he first questioned Mary. Both Mary and Joseph assert their innocence in the matter (15:13, 15). Unconvinced by their testimony, the high priest decides to leave it to God's will to determine their fate by having them both undergo a test involving the drinking of bitter water and being sent into the wilderness (Num 5:11–31; and *m. Sotah* 5.1). After Mary and Joseph pass the test by returning safely, they are cleared of any charges and sent home.

Mary Gives Birth to Jesus

After some unspecified time has passed, but while Mary is still pregnant, a census ordered by King Augustus for all of Judea (cf. Luke 2:1, where the census is for the entire world) requires Mary and Joseph to travel to Bethlehem to register (17:1). The basic story line proceeds with other scenes from canonical Gospel accounts, including the birth of Jesus, the visit from the Magi, and King Herod's attempt to locate and kill Jesus who has been prophesied to unseat him. The *Protevangelium's* repackaging of the account, however, sets the scenes on a new and more vivid stage. While preparing for their travels Joseph contemplates how he should enroll Mary, underscoring their untraditional relationship: "How shall I register her? As my wife? I'm too ashamed to do that. As my daughter? The children of Israel know that she is not my daughter" (17:2–3). With both the appearance of his son Samuel (17:5) as a reminder that Joseph already has children and the repeated references to Mary as a child (17:2), Joseph's role as guardian rather than husband is again highlighted. While en route to Bethlehem, Mary undergoes a prophetic experience in which she sees two peoples, one lamenting and the other rejoicing, most likely representing those who will not accept Jesus' role in salvation history (i.e., the Jews) and those who will (i.e., "Christians") (17:9). Whereas Luke's infancy narrative has Mary give birth in Bethlehem, in the *Prote-vangelium* Mary starts experiencing contractions before they reach the town, thus forcing her to give birth in a cave outside of Bethlehem. After leaving his sons to guard and care for her, Joseph ventures out to locate a Hebrew midwife to help with the delivery. At this point in the narrative a major shift occurs not only in content, but also in writing style: Joseph experiences and relays in the first person a vision in which everything is suspended in time: "I . . . was walking, and yet I was not walking" (18:3); "the ones chewing were not chewing; and the ones lifting up something to eat were not lifting it up" (18:6). This interruption in time signifies the exact moment Jesus enters into the world.

When the suspension of time breaks, the narrative returns to Joseph's search for a midwife. Upon finding one, Joseph engages in an awkward exchange with her over the status and relationship he has with Mary: "Then who is the one who has given birth in a cave? My betrothed . . . Is she not your wife? . . . She is Mary, the one who was brought up in the temple of the Lord . . . I received her by lot as my wife . . . she has conceived by the Holy Spirit . . . " (19:5–9). The two finally make it back just in time to see a cloud overshadowing the cave, and an intense, bright light within the cave that recedes to reveal Mary with Jesus already nursing at her breast (cf. 5:9 when Anna waits the prescribed days). While the midwife is too late to help with the delivery, she does, however, help with attesting to the miraculous events that unfolded: "My soul has been magnified today because my eyes have seen an incredible sign . . . a virgin has given birth" (19:14–18). When a second midwife named Salome appears on the scene, the first unnamed midwife confesses to all that has transpired, but her testimony does not convince Salome. Requiring physical proof, Salome instructs Mary to position herself for a gynecological examination, in which Salome literally attempts to insert her fingers into Mary (20:2–4). The incompatibility of the sacred (Mary's genitals) and the profane (Salome's hand) results in the combustion of Salome's hand (20:4). Immediately recognizing that this is punishment for her transgression and disbelief in the virgin birth, Salome calls out to the God of her fathers, Abraham, Isaac, and Jacob, and begs for forgiveness (20:5–7). Salome finds relief when an angel appears instructing her to hold the child if she wants to seek not just forgiveness, but also salvation and joy (20:9). After she is healed, Salome leaves the cave a believer, but is told not to report on any of what happened until the child goes to Jerusalem (20:12).

The Magi Pay Homage to Mary and Jesus

One of the last sections of the narrative follows the Magi who cause a commotion in Judea with their inquiry about the identity and whereabouts of the new king of the Jews (Matt 2:1–18). Like Matthew's account, the *Protevangelium* attests to the Magi seeing a star in the East and following it because they seek the identity of the messiah as prophesied in the Jewish Scriptures (21:2). However, while Matthew reports that the star stopped at a house in Bethlehem "over the place where the child was" (Matt 2:9), the *Protevangelium* relates that the star from the East led them to the cave (21:10–11). In both accounts, the Magi approach and offer pouches of gold, frankincense-tree, and myrrh before Mary, who is identified in the *Protevangelium* for the first time as a mother (21:11). Both accounts include advice to Joseph and Mary not to go home via Judea since they will encounter Herod's wrath; however, this message is sent by dream in Matt 2:12, but delivered by an angel in the *Protevangelium* (21:12). Herod responds to being tricked by the Magi by sending out his henchmen to kill all children two years old and younger. This element of Matthew's story is expanded and given a colorful new life in the *Protevangelium*, where Jesus' life is saved not by Joseph's flight into Egypt (Matt 2:13–15), but through Mary's quick wit and courage to wrap her child in swaddling clothes and hide him in an ox-manger (22:3–4; cf. Luke 2:7).

Herod's Wrath, Zechariah, and the Epilogue

The remainder of the scene has no parallels in the canonical Gospels. Elizabeth's son John is also in danger because of Herod's threat. Finding no place to hide her son, Elizabeth heads to the mountains to escape the executioners, but when exhaustion prevents her from continuing on, she calls out to the Lord for help; the Lord responds by splitting open the mountain to conceal her (22:5–9). While Elizabeth is able to escape with her son, the fate of her husband is not so bright. Approached by Herod's henchmen at the temple where Zechariah serves as a priest, he is questioned about his son's whereabouts. When Zechariah provides no useful information, he is slain at the altar of the temple and his blood is said to have turned into stone (24:9). The narrative concludes with the priest entering the temple to find only dried blood at the altar but no body, the lamenting of Zechariah's murder, and the appointment of Simeon as Zechariah's replacement (24:4–14). A brief epilogue ends the *Protevangelium* with information about James, the brother of Jesus, the supposed author, and the circumstances surrounding the composition of his account—namely, that he was inspired and given wisdom to write the account during Herod's reign when there was an uproar in Jerusalem (25:1–4) following Herod's death and his son Archelaus's subsequent rise to power.

Title

Despite the testimony of the epilogue, the "Protevangelium of James" is neither the original nor the ancient title of the text; over its long and complicated history it has gone by many different names. In 1552, when Guillaume Postel reintroduced the book to the West,[12] he called the work, *Protevangelium sive de natalibus Jesu Christi et ipsius Matris virginis Mariae, sermo historicus divi Jacobi minoris* (*The Proto-Gospel or the Births of Jesus Christ and His Virgin Mother Mary, A Historical Discourse of Saint James, the Less*), based on a Greek manuscript that has since been lost.[13] The *Protevangelium Jacobi* (or James, as in standard English translation for the Jacobs of the New Testament) is a shortened version of this Latin title. There has been some discussion over whether Postel lifted the title verbatim from the manuscript or whether he simply offered a rendering of it; the latter seems more likely since no other manuscripts attest to this title. The various extant manuscripts only complicate the situation further given that there are a variety of long and confusing titles given to this work. For example, one title reads, "Narrative and History concerning How the Very Holy Mother of God was Born for Our Salvation" (Paris, Bibliothèque nationale de France, gr. 1454) and another, "Narrative of the Holy Apostle James, the Archbishop of Jerusalem and Brother of God, concerning the Birth of the All Holy Mother of God and the Eternal Virgin Mary" (Venice, Biblioteca Nazionale Marciana, II, 82).[14] The Bodmer Miscellaneous Codex, our earliest manuscript of the text dating from the third or fourth century,[15] provides the simple title, "Birth of Mary, Apoc-

12. The *Protevangelium*'s claim that Jesus' "brothers" were sons from Joseph's previous marriage was condemned by Jerome, who argued influentially that these siblings were his cousins (*Helv.* 11–16). Jerome's reasoning was connected to his ascetic position that held that Joseph too was a perpetual virgin. As a result, the *Protevangelium* was condemned by Popes Damascus and Innocent I and then by the Gelasian decree in the sixth century. On the tracing of the *Protevangelium*'s reentrance to the West, see Bouwsma, *Concordia Mundi*, 16–17 and 36. Also helpful is Backus's fuller discussion of Postel's translation in "Guillaume Postel."

13. For a list of other known titles, see Daniels, "Greek Manuscript Tradition," 2–6 (which gives 70 variations); Zervos, "Prolegomena," 2–4 provides 30 more.

14. Tischendorf, *Evangelia Apocrypha*, 1–2; Ehrman and Pleše, *Apocryphal Gospels*, 32.

15. Those convinced by the earlier third-century date include, e.g., Testuz, *Papyrus Bodmer V*, 22; and Vanden Eykel, *Looking Up*, 18. Cullmann ("Protevangelium of James," 421) and Klauck (*Apocryphal Gospels*, 65) have opted for the later fourth-century date. Against general consensus, Raithel ("Beginning at the End," 1) dates

alypse of James,"[16] and even still, it is doubtful that the second half of the title is original,[17] though the attribution to James is fairly common in the manuscript tradition. Several possible early witnesses exist for this text,[18] but only one offers a title for the work. In his commentary on Matthew, Origen of Alexandria (ca. 185–254) refers to Jesus' brother as Joseph's son from a previous marriage and states that his source is either the "Gospel of Peter" or the "Book of James" (*Comm. Matt.* 10:17 on Matt 13:55).[19] It is possible that the *Protevangelium* was originally known very plainly as the "Book of James."

The *Protevangelium of James*[20] and the *Infancy Gospel of James*[21] or *Proto-Gospel of James*[22] are the most widely used contemporary titles for this work,[23] an odd circumstance since neither reference Mary, despite the

---

the manuscript to the end of the second century. For recent studies on the Bodmer Miscellaneous Codex, see Nongbri, "Construction of the Bodmer," 171–72. Working against inadequate descriptions of the manuscript provided by the earliest editors and the lack of quality in the photographing of plates and facsimiles, Nongbri has been making some important advances on the codicological makeup of the Bodmer Papyri.

16. The term "apocalypse" in the title is a reference to the manner in which the narrative was received—that is, through divine revelation—not to a designation of the text to the literary genre of "apocalypse."

17. De Strycker, *La forme la plus ancienne*, 211–12.

18. For other possible witnesses see the section on dating below.

19. Origen's double title is curious. The extant texts of the *Protevangelium* and the *Gospel of Peter* fragments do not share direct parallels; the *Protevangelium*'s primary interest is the life of Mary, while the *Gospel of Peter* focuses on Jesus' death and resurrection. Kraus's and Nicklas's work on the alleged Greek manuscripts of the *Gospel of Peter* contends that it is almost impossible to know exactly what it contained because it is so fragmentary (*Das Petrusevangelium und die Petrusapokalypse*, 3–8, 16). If Origen actually meant the *Gospel of Peter*, then one must be open to the possibility that the *Gospel of Peter* contained a nativity section of some sort.

20. Used by Elliott, "Protevangelium of James," 57–67; Cameron, 'Protevangelium of James," 109–21; Cullmann, "Protevangelium of James," 426–37 (though he adds: "The Birth of Mary [The History of James]," etc.).

21. Used by Hock, *Infancy Gospels*, 1–81; Hock, "Infancy Gospel of James"; Miller, "Infancy Gospel of James," 373–89, etc.

22. Used by Ehrman, "Proto-Gospel of James," 63–72; Ehrman and Pleše, "Proto-Gospel of James, the Birth of Mary, the Revelation of James," 31–71. Cowper uses, "Gospel of James," but also adds in parentheses: "Commonly called the Protevangelium of James. The Birth of Mary, the Holy Mother of God and Very Glorious Mother of Jesus Christ," 3–27.

23. Vorster ("Intertextuality," 270–71) questions the intentionality of the titles and notes that the "Protevangelium" title focuses on the birth of Jesus whereas the "Birth of Mary" highlights Mary's birth.

fact that the text is essentially her biography—all activities and conversations that take place in the narrative are connected to her in some way. More problematic with these two popular titles is that they seem to imply they are something that they are not. The implication of "Protevangelium" is that it is a gospel of sorts. The gospel genre traditionally involves content from the life and ministry of Jesus, which is simply not found in this text. While the pre-script "proto-" is accurate in its suggestion that the text precedes what is found in the canonical gospels, the implication that it is a gospel is still problematic since Jesus appears only at the end of the account and for only brief moments at his birth and infancy. The fully English title, *Infancy Gospel of James* or the *Proto-Gospel of James*, runs into similar problems because it implies a similarity in content and style to other writings categorized as infancy gospels, which again are traditionally about Jesus. While Jesus does make an appearance at the end, the crux and overarching concern is for Mary.[24] Indeed the birth of Jesus and the minor activities associated with his infancy serve primarily to elevate Mary and her exceptional status and condition.

While there is a clear case for why the title of our text should be changed, the traditional title in its semi-anglicized form, the *Protevangelium of James*, will be used here mostly for the sake of convenience; it is popularly and widely used[25] and changing it will only contribute to confusion about its already complicated history, which offers no clear indication of its original form.

Date

General consensus assigns a mid-second century to early third-century date to the text. While dates as late as the fifth century were proposed at the beginning of the twentieth century, these proposals were debunked with the discovery of the third- or fourth-century Bodmer Miscellanous Codex in 1952, which serves as our earliest manuscript of the *Protevangelium*.[26] In support of the earlier dating of the text scholars have looked

24. Cf. Toepel (*Protevangelium*, 38–41, 269–70) who argues that the text should be categorized as an infancy gospel because its goals are primarily to praise the miraculous deeds of a god (i.e., Jesus).

25. E.g., Elliott, *Apocryphal New Testament*, 48–67; Cameron, *Other Gospels*, 107–21; Vuong, *Gender and Purity*; Gregory and Tuckett, eds., *Early Christian Apocrypha*.

26. Note that this earliest manuscript also shows signs of secondary developments, i.e., omissions, editing, etc. See de Strycker, *La forme la plus ancienne*, 13–18.

for indications of knowledge of the text in the works of early church writers.[27] As noted above, Origen (ca. 185–254) cites a "Book of James" or the "Gospel of Peter" as a source for the tradition that Joseph was previously married and had children before his engagement to Mary (*Comm. Matt.* 10.17). This belief is articulated several times throughout the narrative: Joseph's protest against taking on Mary is based on his already having children (*Prot. Jas.* 9:9); Joseph makes reference to his sons and specifically names Samuel as one of his children when contemplating how he will register for the upcoming census (17:2); and Joseph leaves his sons to care for Mary while he searches for a midwife (18:1). Clement (ca. 150–215), an older contemporary of Origen, mentions the tradition of a midwife who aids Mary at the birth and attests to her *virginitas in partu* (*Strom.* 7.16). Although Clement does not provide a source for this knowledge, he does relay that it is a widely held belief by most people. Other witnesses to Mary's post-partum virginity include Irenaeus of Lyon (*Epid.* 54), Ignatius of Antioch (*Eph.* 19.1), the *Ascension of Isaiah* 11:1–16, and the *Odes of Solomon* 19.[28] Finally, the Carthaginian author Tertullian (ca. 160–225) vehemently refutes Mary's eternal virginity (*non virgo quantum a partu*; *Carn. Chr.* 23) as well as the possibility that Jesus' brothers and sisters were Joseph's children from a previous marriage (*Carn. Chr.* 7).

P. A. van Stempvoort has drawn on additional evidence to propose a precise date of composition between 178 and 204 CE.[29] The *terminus a quo* of ±178 CE is based on van Stempvoort's reading of Celsus's *True Doctrine* (preserved in Origen's *Contra Celsum*), which attacks Mary's character most viciously. Celsus questions the legitimacy of Mary's virginity, respected lineage, high social background, and livelihood. Reading the *Protevangelium* as an apology, van Stempvoort asserts that the text functioned specifically to counter these slanders. For example, he cites the *Protevangelium*'s reference to Mary's wealth and royal lineage as a rebuttal of Celsus's accusation that Mary was a poor village girl who had

27. Discussion in Hock, *Infancy Gospels*, 11; van Stempvoort, "Protevangelium Jacobi," 415; Foster, "Protevangelium of James," 576, de Strycker, *La forme la plus ancienne*, 418; Vuong, *Gender and Purity*, 32–33.

28. Note that Mary's virginity post-partum is only implied in Ignatius's letter (see section on Provenance below). To Mary's post-partum virginity, Irenaeus also seems to suggest that the birthing experience was painless and caused no bodily damage. For further discussion, see Plumpe, "Some Little-Known Early Witnesses"; Buck, "Witnesses to an Early Cult of Mary"; and Vuong, *Gender and Purity*, 218–22.

29. Van Stempvoort, "Protevangelium Jacobi," 410–26.

to spin for a living (*Cels.* 1.28–32). His highly scandalous accusation that Mary's child, born in secret, was the product of an adulterous relationship with a Roman soldier named Panthera (*Cels.* 1.32) is countered by the emphatic statements and physical proof of her maintained virginity found throughout the *Protevangelium*. Van Stempvoort adds that Origen knew a *Biblos Iakobou* and that many of his contemporaries had knowledge of the *Protevangelium*'s content, thus strengthening the earliest possible date of 178 CE. For his specific *terminus ad quem* date of 204 CE, Van Stempvoort looks to Hippolytus's homily on Susanna (in *Comm. Dan.*). Seeing strong parallels between the depiction of Susanna and the two major female figures in the *Protevangelium*, he suggests that the parallels are indicative of a shared compositional time period. Van Stempvoort's incredibly precise dating may give some readers pause,[30] but his proposal shines important light on sources that may indicate knowledge of the *Protevangelium*. If Origen's, Clement's, and Tertullian's source for all these unique details is indeed the *Protevangelium*, its *terminus ad quem* can be placed reasonably at the beginning of the third century CE.

Another ambitious attempt at dating the text has been made by George Zervos who has proposed a very early date based on his determination of a literary dependency between the *Protevangelium* and Justin Martyr (d. 160), who makes reference to Mary giving birth in a cave outside of Bethlehem (*1 Apol.* 1.33). Zervos proposes a date no later than 150–160, the period in which Justin was actively writing, and a date no earlier than 80–90 when Matthew and Luke were discussing the virgin birth.[31] Zervos's argument is based in part on the work of Émile de Strycker, who suggested that the *Protevangelium* knew Justin's work grounded on four concordances he found between the two texts.[32] Zervos reverses the direction of dependency.[33] While Zervos has not been able to persuade many, his theory is intriguing and speaks to the range of proposed dates for our text.

30. Hock has argued that it is too ambitious and relies too heavily on the assumption that the text is an apology. See also Zervos, "Dating the Protevangelium of James," 415–34 and Vuong, *Gender and Purity*, 37.

31. Zervos, "Dating the Protevangelium," 419.

32. For de Strycker's four concordances and his conclusions on the connection between the *Protevangelium* and Justin Martyr, see *La forme la plus ancienne*, 414 and his later article revising his position in "Protévangile de Jacques," 353.

33. For a detailed explanation of the parallels that have convinced Zervos that Justin relies on the *Protevangelium*, see Zervos, "Dating the Protevangelium of James."

Provenance

The *Protevangelium's* provenance is one of the more debated issues surrounding the text's origin, most likely because it is intricately related to questions regarding its relationship to Judaism (see section on relationship to Judaism below). Frequent dismissals of proposed geographical areas largely depended upon the text's knowledge of Judaism or lack thereof. The problematic assumption that knowledge of "Jewish tradition and customs" would necessitate a Palestinian setting while the lack of this knowledge would require a different location functioned as the dominant determinant for how the text's provenance should be discussed. Diasporic Jews who engaged in pilgrimages to Jerusalem offer a clear example of why such an approach is flawed, inasmuch as such travels gave them intimate knowledge of the geographical space of Jerusalem, despite not being inhabitants of the area.[34]

Other contentious criteria traditionally used for determining locale involve references to or knowledge of geographical and/or environmental details. De Strycker is often cited in this regard, as he rejected Palestine because of the author's apparent confusion about the distance between Jerusalem, Judea, and Bethlehem with regard to Mary's and Joseph's travels. He argues instead for an Egyptian provenance based on linguistic features and the influence of Coptic elements in the author's writing, but also on the description of the mountains and wilderness at *Prot. Jas.* 1:9; 4:5; and 16:4–5, which he argues is characteristic of the geographical landscape of Egypt.[35] Also problematic is the close proximity of the gates of Jerusalem to the desert (*Prot. Jas.* 4:4–5), which persuaded de Strycker even further that the text was not composed in Palestine.[36] É. Cothenet

---

34. Josephus, *B.J.* 6.9.3 [423-26]; see also *t. Pesah.* 5) describes tens of thousands of Jews from the diaspora who would come to Jerusalem especially during important holidays like Passover. On the flip side, this intimate knowledge of Palestinian geography would also be accessible to non-Jews living in Palestine.

35. De Strycker (*La forme la plus ancienne*, 422), writes: "Or cette permutabilité du désert et de la montagne est caractéristique de l'Égypte. La partie habitable du pays consiste dans la plaine alluviale parfaitement unie que couvrent chaque année les inondations du Nil; de part et d'autre s'élèvent les parois rocheuses au-delà desquelles s'étendent des hauts-plateaux désertiques d'une sécheresse absolue. *Montagne* et *désert* sont ici identiques."

36. Again, de Strycker (*La forme la plus ancienne*, 419–21), argues that Egypt's desert, which is immediately bordered by habitable land, makes the author's choice of situating the desert in close proximity to the memorial gates of Jerusalem at *Prot. Jas.* 4:4–5 possible.

also supports Egypt as the place of origin, but his reasoning is based on Origen's and Clement's knowledge of the text.[37]

Not everyone has so readily rejected Palestine as a possible place of composition. Malcolm Lowe reevaluated the passages traditionally viewed as demonstrating ignorance of Palestinian geography and proposed instead an alternative interpretation of the details. He suggests that Joseph's reference to being "in," "near," or "around" Bethlehem before preparing to "depart for Judea" (*Prot. Jas.* 21:1) may be influenced by John 3:22, where Jerusalem is described as distinct from Judea. In this case, Jesus is described as going forth into Judea from Jerusalem. Lowe also offers other examples from Jewish literature (e.g., Ezra 1:2, 1:3, 2:1; *m. Ket.* 4.12), which acknowledge that a distinction can be made between Jerusalem and Judea.[38] In response to the widely accepted proposals by de Strycker over the location of mountains and deserts, Lowe also argues that Palestine cannot be so easily dismissed if one considers the heavy rainfall on the western slopes that would allow for the desert to start on the eastern slopes of the mountains that borders Jerusalem. To further support his claim, Lowe notes that the author calls the people not Ἰουδαῖοι (Judeans), but "Israel," that is, the term commonly used by writers living in Palestine. The only reference to Ἰουδαῖοι is made by one of the Magi, a non-Israelite, in his questioning of Herod over the location of the newborn King of the Jews. While Lowe's investigation offers legitimate pause for the exclusion of Palestine, several scholars have noted that his explanation for Joseph going "from Bethlehem to Judea" at *Prot. Jas.* 21:1 is still not adequate.[39]

While the debate on provenance remains unsettled, perhaps the strongest contender for the text's origin is Syria. Much like the arguments put forth for Egypt, however, traditional proposals have also relied on dubious assumptions about the proposed location's geography and environment. H. R. Smid, for instance, rejected an Egyptian origin because he was unconvinced that the geographical details reflected a specifically Egyptian landscape. Opting for Syria instead, he cites the popular laurel

37. Cothenet, "Protévangile de Jacques," 4267.

38. Lowe, "ΙΟΥΔΑΙΟΙ of the Apocrypha," 62 n.24.

39. Hock, *Infancy Gospels*, 13; Elliott, "Developing Role of Mary," 270–71. Lowe ("ΙΟΥΔΑΙΟΙ of the Apocrypha," 62 n.24) notes that *Prot. Jas.* 21:1 is not as problematic as one may assume since other manuscripts have different wording and do not attest to this error. It is not, in his opinion, sufficient cause to dismiss Jewish authorship.

trees and gardens of Syria as having inspired Anna's garden scene.[40] More recent trends have seen Syria as the more persuasive locale, but the criteria for determining such a conclusion have moved away from geographical details to a focus on literary parallels and the concerns and interests of the texts that may be more popularly reflected there. Ron Cameron notes that the *Protevangelium*'s harmonization techniques parallel the popular use of gospel harmonies in Syria.[41] Drawing comparisons between the *Protevangelium*'s depiction of Mary's unique virginal status and the birth of her child and those found in the second-century writings of the *Ascension of Isaiah* and the *Odes of Solomon*, J. K. Elliott also posits a Syrian provenance.[42] In the case of the *Ascension of Isaiah*, these similarities include the absence of a midwife during the actual birth (*Prot. Jas.* 19:12–16; cf. *Ascen. Isa.* 11:14) and Mary's *virginitas post partum* (*Prot. Jas.* 20:1–3; cf. *Ascen. Isa.* 11:10). Other correspondences between these two texts include the reference to Mary's Davidic descent (*Prot. Jas.* 10:4; cf. *Ascen. Isa.* 11:2), Joseph's depiction as a carpenter (*Prot. Jas.* 9:1; cf. *Ascen. Isa.* 11:2)[43] and the reference to and use of lots or "portions" (*Prot. Jas.* 9:7, 10:7–8; cf. *Ascen. Isa.* 11:3).[44]

Another literary source that strengthens the case for Syria is Ignatius of Antioch's letter to the Ephesians (19.1), which also attests to Mary's virginity *in partu*, albeit it is only implied in that giving birth too did not nullify her status as virgin: "the virginity of Mary and her giving birth eluded the ruler of this age, likewise also the death of the Lord—three mysteries of a cry which were done in the stillness of God."[45] The *Odes*

---

40. Smid (*Protevangelium Jacobi*, 41) also admits that the evidence is inconclusive. His argument builds on the work of Conrady, "Protevangelum Jacobi," 770–72.

41. Cameron (*Other Gospels*, 108–109) also says that Asia Minor, Rome, and Egypt are still possibilities, though he does favor Syria.

42. Elliott, *Apocryphal New Testament*, 49; Elliott, "Developing Role of Mary," 271–72.

43. While the reference to Joseph as a carpenter can be found in Matt 13:55 (and Mark 6:3), it is not a particularly Matthean concept. Enrico Norelli has convincingly argued that the nativity scene in the *Ascension of Isaiah* is independent from the Gospel of Matthew. Note too that the nativity scene in the *Ascension of Isaiah* overall shows great affinity to the *Protevangelium*, suggesting the probability of a literary relationship. See Norelli, *Ascensio Isaiae: Commentarius*, but also the abridged version of the work in *Ascension du prophète Isaïe* and his commentary companion *L'Ascensione di Isaia*.

44. Vuong, *Gender and Purity*, 41–42.

45. Translation from Schoedel, *Ignatius of Antioch*, 87.

of Solomon, another text of Syrian origin, shares with both the *Ascension of Isaiah* and the *Protevangelium* the view that no midwife was present and that Mary seemed to suffer no pain during the delivery of the child (19:6–9). Though literary dependency between the texts may be difficult to prove, the parallels between the texts are too close to be mere coincidences and may suggest a common provenance.

If one takes into consideration the text's overarching themes and concerns, Syria continues to be a leading contender for place of origin. Anti-docetic and anti-Marcionite views, for example, are prominent themes in sources of Syrian provenance. The *Protevangelium*'s detailed description of Mary's pregnant body (12:7, 13:1), descriptions of physical discomfort (17:6–7) coupled with her nursing of Jesus (19:16), and a very corporeal gynecological examination (20:1–2) can be convincingly read as a response to docetic claims that regarded Jesus' body as semblance (as Irenaeus taught of Marcion's beliefs: *Haer* 4.33.2.5) and likened Mary's experience of childbirth "as water through a tube" (Irenaeus on Valentinus: *Haer.* 1.7.2 and 3.11.3). Additionally, while Marcion's docetic ideas are only known to us from his opponents' writings, there is scholarly consensus that his canon excluded the first four chapters of Luke.[46] This rejection of Jesus' conception, genealogy, baptism, and temptation as well as information about his parents and the prediction of his birth (and John's) could be seen as an attempt to sever all human connections and Jewish roots from Jesus. Such as position might readily be countered by the *Protevangelium*'s massive expansion of Mary's upbringing and emphatic Davidic ties.

Additionally, the general Jewish-Christian milieu of Syria is consistent with the presentation of continued Jewish practices and customs in the *Protevangelium*. In particular, Torah observances especially related to the temple and concern for biblical law (especially purity regulations and dietary restrictions), fit in well with the kind of sentiments held by Paul, Matthew, and Ignatius on the appropriate relationship between

46. Tradition holds that Marcion's canon generally consisted of letters by Paul and a mutilated version of Luke. Recent studies, however, have increasingly questioned whether Marcion utilized and adopted rather than edited already-existing forms of documents he viewed as Scripture (e.g., BeDuhn, "Myth of Marcion as Redactor," 15–42). For a reconstruction of Marcion's gospel, see Harnack, *Marcion*, 165–222; BeDuhn, *First New Testament*, 229–59; and Roth, "Marcion's Gospel," 410–36. Despite cautioning against the reliability of the wording in Harnack's reconstruction, Tyson (*Marcion and Luke-Acts*, 43) contends that it is with certainty that Marcion's gospel "lacks an account of Jesus' birth and infancy."

Judaism and Christianity.[47] These three writers, among others, attest to the vehement debates and the complicated relationship between Judaism and Christianity in the early Christian centuries. Some firmly rejected the fluidity between Jewish and Christian traditions and the continued Jewish observances held by some who professed Christ; precisely that same fluidity is promoted within the *Protevangelium*.[48] Thus while a Syrian locale cannot be determined with absolute certainty, it is a highly plausible proposition and presently the most sensible conclusion.

Relationship to Judaism

As mentioned above, the *Protevangelium's* relationship to Judaism is probably the most highly contested issue related to the text's origins, as made evident by the various waves in scholarship for and against a Jewish connection. Early studies on the *Protevangelium* generally assumed a Jewish milieu for the text given its frequent use and deep knowledge of the Septuagint. Not only are names and characters drawn from portrayals of famous figures—including Joachim in Susanna 1–4 and Hannah in 1 Samuel 1:1–28—but Anna's and Joachim's characterizations exhibit clear parallels with the biblical barren couples Sarah and Abraham and Hannah and Elkannah.[49] Van Stempvoort has argued that the stories of these biblical matriarchs and other Hellenistic Jewish sources including Susanna, Tobit, and Judith played a significant role in the crafting of Mary's character in the *Protevangelium*. Moreover, van Stempvoort writes that the text's tone, thought, language, usage, and motifs all point to the Septuagint as a source.[50] Cameron makes a similar appeal, describing the *Protevangelium* as being entirely "steeped in the language of the Septua-

47. The major disputes over circumcision and dietary laws between Peter and Paul found in Acts and parts of Galatians attest to the influence of Judaism in earliest Antiochene Christianity. While Matthew's provenance is contested, Antioch remains the dominant choice for the gospel's origins. Zetterholm contends that even if an Antiochene locale cannot be determined conclusively for Matthew, Ignatius of Antioch "not only knew but used the Gospel of Matthew." At the very least, Matthew's reception can be placed in Antioch; Zetterholm, *Formation of Christianity in Antioch*, 211. See also, Sim, "Matthew and Ignatius of Antioch," 140–41.

48. I have argued elsewhere (*Gender and Purity*, 195–223) for a Syrian provenance based on the criteria of Syria's deep concern for anti-docetic and anti-Marcionite literature, and for Jewish-Christian influences.

49. Hock, *Infancy Gospels*, 25–26.

50. Van Stempvoort, "Protevangelium Jacobi," 415–19.

gint" not only in terms of its use of individual words and phrases, but also in style.[51]

In line with de Strycker, who also supported a Jewish milieu for the text, Smid was so persuaded by the parallels he saw between the text and the Septuagint that he offered a detailed proposal for the profile of the author: someone of Jewish descent born after the destruction of the Jerusalem temple in 70 CE or someone who was highly influenced by and/or had extensive knowledge of the Septuagint and the Hebrew Bible.[52] Like Cameron and van Stempvoort, Smid saw the *Protevangelium* as heavily couched in the same thought and vocabulary of the Septuagint. To make his point, Smid notes various examples in which unique Septuagintal phrases like "the great day of the Lord" (ἡ ἡμέρα χυρίου ἡ μεγάλη; 1:4) and practices like the bitter water test administered by the temple priest (5:1) are used at pivotal points in the narrative.[53]

However, when these Jewish elements were scrutinized further, many of the parallels found in the *Protevangelium* did not seem to line up as closely with the Hebrew Bible in terms of its literature, traditions, rituals, and customs. Cullmann,[54] Elliott,[55] and Hock,[56] among others,[57] stress that a number of the Jewish traditions depicted in the *Protevangelium* are distorted representations of Jewish practices, including Joachim's rejection at the temple because of his childlessness (1:5), Mary's upbringing at the temple (7:1—9:10), and Joseph's travels *to* Judea *from* Bethlehem (since Bethlehem is already in Judea) (21:1) as either being unknown practices or a misunderstanding of Jewish customs.[58] With regard to misunderstanding Jewish traditions, the bitter water test (16:3) is perhaps the most widely referenced. Numbers 5:11–31, in which such a test is given

---

51. Cameron, *Other Gospels*, 108.

52. Smid, *Protevangelium Jacobi*, 9–12.

53. Smid, *Protevangelium Jacobi*, 21.

54. Cullmann, "Protevangelium of James," 423–24.

55. Elliott, *Apocryphal New Testament*, 49 and Elliott, "Developing Role of Mary," 270–71.

56. While Hock also argues that the parallels between the Septuagint are undeniable, he adds: "indeed the author himself hardly came from a Jewish milieu, as there are not only problems with Palestinian geography but also little knowledge of Jewish life and customs that does not come from the Septuagint" (*Infancy Gospels*, 10).

57. See also Pratscher, *Herrenbruder Jakobus*, 224.

58. Elliott, *Apocryphal New Testament*, 49; and Elliott, "Developing Role of Mary," 271; Cullmann, "Protevangelium of James," 423–24.

to a wife who is suspected of adultery, is cited as the source of this scene. Upon drinking the bitter water and swearing an oath, two outcomes are possible to determine the loyalty of the accused wife: if she is innocent, nothing will happen and she will be able to bear children, but if she is guilty, she will experience immediate physical pain, whereby her uterus will drop and her womb will discharge. The punishment for swearing falsely, therefore, is the removal of the accused woman's ability to have children. Elliott notes that the bitter water scene in the *Protevangelium* does not correspond with the test described in Numbers as both Mary and Joseph are required to take the test to determine whether the two consummated the marriage (a marriage arranged specifically by the same priests, no less).[59] Numbers also offers other details including the tousling of the woman's hair and a recitation of a curse formula. The intention and details of the bitter water test in Numbers, according to Elliott, are simply not present in the *Protevangelium*.

Michael Mach also dismisses the possibility of a Jewish or Jewish-Christian origin for the *Protevangelium* but for different reasons.[60] Mach argues that etymological wordplays that have been used to justify possible connections to Judaism are in fact expressions that have been lifted from the Septuagint or the NT and cannot be used as evidence for any real connection between the text and Judaism.[61] In addition, he is not persuaded by the argument that Mary's appointment to weaving the temple veil has a halakhic basis, or rather knowledge of Jewish customs, because of the emphasis on her exceptional purity and virginity as the reason for her selection. He argues instead that this detail is not a uniquely Jewish custom given that various temples in Athens also required the purity of all workers.[62]

Those willing to see some possibility of a Jewish background for the text have reasonably looked for other expressions of early Judaism beyond simply the Septuagint and Hebrew Bible. Taking advantage of the fact that Judaism was highly diverse and that the formation of Jewish and Christian identities was still very fluid in the first few centuries CE, such scholars have contributed to new trends that do not so easily dismiss the Judaism question. W. S. Vorster, for example, explores the representation

59. Frymer-Kensky, "Strange Case of the Suspected Sotah," 11–26.

60. Mach, "Are There Jewish Elements," 215–22.

61. Mach, "Are There Jewish Elements," 220.

62. Mach, "Are There Jewish Elements," 216–17.

of the Jews in the text to nuance the approach for understanding the text's relationship with Judaism. Noting that identifiably Christian texts often portrayed Jews in negative ways and Jewish customs and traditions as being superseded, Vorster finds that the Jewish leadership, people, and institutions are simply not portrayed in that way.[63] He writes that Jewish leaders in particular are unexpectedly doing all the right things: they are helpers of the protagonist and the message of the text by offering blessings (17:3, et al.), praying (8:3 et al.), correctly performing rituals and rites (6:2; 8:2, 3; 24:1, et al.), and taking care of the temple and determining proper practices and norms (10:1; 15:3 et al.). Their authority and acts are also legitimized and verified by God as illustrated by the divine responses to questions and advice asked of him (8:3–8; 9:3–6). Vorster argues that even when Jewish leadership aggressively demands the testing of Mary and Joseph via the bitter water test, they still continue to support and contribute to the message of the *Protevangelium* in that Mary and Joseph are declared unequivocally to be innocent and pure. For all these reasons, Vorster suggests that the author likely had Jewish interests when crafting his story about Mary.

Cothenet also offers a proposal that reconsiders the text's relationship with Judaism by expanding what constitutes Judaism in the first centuries CE. Describing the *Protevangelium* as one of the "premier midrash chrétien sur la Nativité de Marie," Cothenet draws a number of parallels between the traditions depicted in the *Protevangelium* and the Jewish scriptures and stories found within rabbinic tradition.[64] He also proposes that many of the *Protevangelium*'s motifs were influenced by those found in the Haggadah. Timothy Horner follows suit in this reevaluation by looking into rabbinic literature, but his approach is more careful in that he limits his sources to tannaitic traditions. He writes boldly that the "*Prot. Jas.* would have been best understood—perhaps only fully understood—within a community that was familiar with concerns and images of contemporary Judaism."[65] Past rejection of the text's relationship to Judaism, according to Horner, was based on a disconnection between the *Protevangelium* and elements characteristic of Second Temple Jewish, pre-rabbinic literature.

---

63. Vorster, "Annunciation of the Birth," 41.

64. Cothenet, "Protévangile de Jacques," 4252.

65. Horner, "Jewish Aspects," 317.

Horner's most intriguing proposal is that some of the *Protevange-lium*'s major themes—including childlessness, betrothal, marriage, and virginity—are more fruitfully read in the context of ideas found in the Mishnah.[66] For instance, he argues that Mary's life can be divided into three stages: birth to age three, ages three to twelve, and from twelve to adulthood—corresponding to the life cycle of girls found in the Mishnah. Specifically, *m. Nid.* 5.4 and *m. Ket.* 1.1–3 describe the parameters of virginity loss; namely, the virginity of a girl three years and a day or younger can be assured, whereas the virginity of a girl older than three years and a day cannot.[67] For Horner, this mishnaic tradition offers insight into why Anna and Joachim decide to dedicate their daughter at the age of three instead of their initial plan to send her to the temple at the age of two. Even more, Horner takes up the highly contested bitter water test scene arguing that the *Protevangelium*'s version is more aligned with the mishnaic discussion of the Sotah than with Numbers 5:11–31 since the former describes a test to determine fidelity by acting as a sort of truth-telling serum.[68] In the *Protevangelium*, Mary *and* Joseph are required to take the test because both are being questioned about their actions; additionally, the test is not used to determine an illegitimate pregnancy.

While Horner's proposal has been criticized given that his approach attempts to connect the text with the Mishnah, an early third-century collection which has no historical evidence of exerting influence in the second century, his point is well taken that the parallels between the *Protevangelium* and the Mishnah help to reevaluate the text's relationship with Judaism, even if no direct relationship can be determined. Horner's study also helps problematize the questions concerning categories. Describing the difficulty of determining the influence of Jewish Scriptures on apocryphal literature more generally, Tobias Nicklas asserts that much of the struggle has to do with the fact that while one can locate intertextual relationships between apocryphal writings and what we now know as the Hebrew Bible or the Old Testament, "there was no fixed Jewish 'canon' (in the sense of a fixed list of writings)—neither in the form of a Tanak nor as 'the' Septuagint."[69] Nicklas's comments generally construed remind us of the fluidity and murkiness of categories and boundaries

---

66. Horner, "Jewish Aspects," 318–29.

67. Horner, "Jewish Aspects," 321–24.

68. Horner, "Jewish Aspects," 328–29.

69. Nicklas, "Influence of Jewish Scriptures," 141.

related to Jewish and Christian literature and identities in the first few centuries of the Common Era, the period in which general consensus holds our text to have been written. These ideas concretely problematize the position that the *Protevangelium* has no real connections to Judaism.

Genre, Purpose, and Possible Audience

The *Protevangelium*'s genre, purpose, and even possible audience are closely connected to the text's overarching goals. Scholarship on the text has proposed a number of reasons for its creation including, "filling in gaps," "expanding," and "interpreting" the writings of the New Testament (see also the section on sources below).[70] In many ways, the *Protevangelium* does fill in gaps by providing its readers with rich and detailed descriptions of an incredibly prominent woman in Christian history, but for whom we receive precious little information in the canonical Gospels about her character, history, or background. Some have suggested that the popularity of infancy gospels (cf. the section on title above) inspired interest in creating literature about the early life of Mary, a process that ultimately developed into a need to provide her with her own biography. Many have read the *Protevangelium* as a vital part of the ancient biographical genre that sought to better understand and to help quench the desire to know more about the lives of the "rich and famous."

Another popular genre of literature among early Christians, especially prior to Constantine, was apologetics. As a tradition that had not yet gained complete legitimacy throughout the Roman Empire, Christianity felt the need to craft writings that were apologetic in nature or at least had apologetic aims. The *Protevangelium*'s specific claim that Mary conceived and gave birth as a virgin seems to respond to various Jewish and/or "pagan" polemics against Mary. A number of scholars have argued that the work shows clear signs of being motivated by apologetic concerns.[71] Van Stempvoort takes this proposal a step further by suggesting the text is specifically intended to counter Celsus's attacks on Mary. He views the

70. See Klauck, *Apocryphal Gospels*, 64; Hock, *Infancy Gospels*, 3; Elliott, *Apocryphal New Testament*, 46; Cullmann, "Protevangelium of James," 414–18. The purpose of apocryphal literature in general also has been described in this way; see e.g., Gregory and Tuckett, ed. *Early Christian Apocrypha*, 6.

71. Klauck, *Apocryphal Gospels*, 66; Allen, "Protevangelium of James as 'Historia,'" 515–17; Smid, *Protevangelium Jacobi*, 15–17; Cothenet, "Protévangile de Jacques," 4268; Elliott, *Apocryphal New Testament*," 49–50; and Horner, "Jewish Aspects," 330.

specific details of Mary's proven and enduring purity and virginity, the description of her parents as wealthy and respected members of the community (1:1–3), and Mary's weaving of the temple curtain (12:1) as direct responses to Celsus's accusations that Mary had a child out of wedlock with a Roman solider, was the daughter of poor and socially insignificant parents, and that she spun for a living.[72]

Galit Hasan-Rokem traces the roots of Celsus's polemic to folkloric Jewish tradition that may have begun in the first century.[73] Two rabbinic references come to mind that offer some parallels. In the Tosefta (*t. Hull.* 2.22–24) there is a reference to a "Yeshu ben Panthera" who might be a thinly-veiled Jesus given that various versions of the illegitimate birth of Jesus claimed he was the son of a Roman soldier named Panthera. In the later traditions of *b. San.* 106a, there is also a reference to an unnamed woman who is described as playing the "harlot with carpenters"—a possible reference to Mary given Joseph's frequent association with carpentry. That the *Protevangelium* repeatedly affirms Mary's virginity by having a number of different and independent witnesses—including the angel (11:5–8), Joseph (14:5), the priest and people of Israel (16:5–8), an unnamed midwife (19:14), and Salome (20:1–2, 10)—attest to her certainly indicates an attempt to refute any slanderous and defamatory remarks made against her character. Bart Ehrman and Zlatko Pleše remind us, too, that doctrinal debates and theological discussions about Mary's purity and eternal virginity, which occupied various councils from the fourth century and beyond, were rooted in the *Protevangelium*'s apologetic discourse.[74]

The incredibly flattering depiction of Mary in the *Protevangelium* has encouraged Hock to suggest another possible reason for its creation. Namely, Hock reads the consistent praising of Mary as an encomium consistent with the Greco-Roman standards of literature written with the purpose to praise. While he does not deny that the narrative serves apologetic concerns, he asserts that it "hardly needs to be the principal purpose [and] does not explain the gospel as a whole."[75] Indeed, the *Protevangelium*'s overwhelming focus on Mary's purity greatly exceeds any proof needed to defend accusations made against her status. To offer

72. Van Stempvoort, "Protevangelium Jacobi," 410.

73. Hasan-Roken, *Web of Life*, 156.

74. Ehrman and Pleše, *Apocryphal Gospels*, 35.

75. Hock, *Infancy Gospels*, 15.

support, Hock compares the text with the expectations of Hermogenes' *Progymnasmata* to argue that the *Protevangelium* was crafted and guided with these criteria in mind. As a teaching manual, the *Progymnasmata* provides instructions and examples of common characteristics for encomium writing. Family, national origin, upbringing, achievements, and virtuous deeds are several aspects commonly found in Greco-Roman encomiums, all of which Hock sees as being directly addressed in the *Protevangelium*.[76] Consistent with Hock's claim, Mary Foskett argues that the driving force behind the narrative is "praise of Mary—rather than the need to defend her."[77]

The deliberate focus on Mary and her extraordinary features has also convinced Stephen Shoemaker that the main motivation of the text must be the extolling of Mary for her own sake, rather than, for example, Christological reasons that sought to confirm Jesus' divinity though his mother's virginal birth. No doubt, the *Protevangelium* addresses these concerns by making clear that Jesus was truly born of a virgin, but the narrative's focus is wholly devoted to Mary;[78] indeed Jesus seldom appears and only in the context of his mother giving birth to him. Mary no longer functions as the protagonist in the final section of the narrative (22–25), but Jesus is absent also. The reality of Jesus' virgin birth need not require an entire book to demonstrate what can easily be made plain in a single chapter.

Authorship, Sources, and Literary Unity

The epilogue of the *Protevangelium* attributes the work to James, the brother of Jesus and the bishop of Jerusalem (Matt 13:55; Mark 6:3; Gal 1:19; Acts 15:13–21) and sets the time of its composition during the period in which Herod was king of Judea (25:1–4). The *Protevangelium*,

76. Perhaps one obstacle facing Hock's proposal comes from the text, which describes itself as a "historia" (25:1). To this hurdle, Hock (*Infancy Gospels*, 15–20) proposes that the *Protevangelium* is a "historical narrative" with encomiastic views, and that while it may not have been the encomiastic as envisioned by the *Progymnasmata*, its form and structure, if not its self-description, reflects an encomium agenda.

77. Foskett, "Virginity as Purity," 68. See also Vuong, *Gender and Purity*, 54–57.

78. Norelli (*Marie des Apocryphes*, 76–78) argues that the desire to confirm Jesus' divine origin via his mother's virgin birth is equally achievable if the narrative focused on Joseph instead, reinforcing the idea that the attention to Mary is intentional. Shoemaker (*Mary in Early Christian Faith*, 55) points to a Latin "special source" that features Joseph in a similar manner and was used by later Latin and Irish apocrypha.

however, is a pseudonymous work and as such, its authorship, as well as date and provenance are difficult to determine with precision and have spurred some debate among modern scholars. While more recent trends in apocrypha scholarship have cautioned against offering exact identities about authors and intended readers/audiences,[79] especially based on approaching texts through "mirror reading,"[80] some general inferences can certainly be made of the author's educational exposure and cultural background. For example, like Matthew and Luke, the author has a clear knowledge of the Septuagint, as evident in the close affinities between the depiction of Mary and the biblical matriarchs including Sarah (Gen 18, 20–21) and Hannah (1 Sam 1–2) mentioned above, but also because the tone, thought, language, usages, and motifs found in the *Protevangelium* resemble Septuagint texts too closely to be coincidental.[81] Other Hellenistic Jewish sources such as Susanna (Dan 13:1–64), Tobit, and Judith also seem to have a deep influence on the *Protevangelium* in terms of style and motifs.

Literary elements and social conventions from Greco-Roman romances also have been detected in the *Protevangelium*. In particular, Hock has argued that Anna's lament in the garden (3:2–8), Joseph's wailing in response to Mary's condition (13:1–5), and the bitter water test (16:3–8) all parallel the style, language, and motifs found in the Greek romances of Longus's *Daphnis and Chloe* and Achilles Tatius's *Leucippe and Clitophon*.[82] In the former case, Daphnis's lament also takes place in a garden (4.28.3). In Achilles Tatius's novel, Clitophon expresses a lament closely resembling Joseph's (5.11.3) and Leucippe is also required to take a water test to prove her purity (8.3.3; 6.1–5; 13.1—14.2). Furthermore, Hock argues that certain Greco-Roman conventions may also help understand details that would be understood easily by the audience of the *Protevangelium*, but might be lost on a modern reader. For example, he cites Chloe's discussion with her mother Nape, who warns that her virginity might be more safeguarded at home spinning rather than out frolicking on the hillsides, as an aid to understanding why Mary rushes home to her threads upon hearing a bodiless voice (*Prot. Jas.* 11:1–4).

79. For a discussion on the intended reader in antiquity and also specifically of the *Protevangelium*, see Vanden Eykel, *Looking Up*, 46–56.

80. See esp. Hurtado, "Who Read Early Christian Apocrypha," 153–66.

81. Hock, *Infancy Gospels*, 25–26; van Stempvoort, "Protevangelium Jacobi," 415–19.

82. Hock, *Infancy Gospels*, 25–27.

For Hock, Greek novels share with the *Protevangelium* a deep concern for sexual purity, providing insight not only into the intentions of the writing but also, by implication, the audience who valued and "read" these works.

Questions regarding specific sources for the text have also proven difficult to answer. Given that the *Protevangelium* can be divided into three main parts and at two points the narrative switches to the first person (chaps. 18 and 25), albeit with two different first person voices, has led some to suspect multiple sources. At the end of the nineteenth century Adolf von Harnack was the first to suggest the *Protevangelium* was a composite text when he posited three independent sources each with differing dates of composition: a biography of Mary's nativity, which informed the beginning of the text's description of her lineage, miraculous birth, upbringing by her parents and the temple priests, engagement to Joseph, and conception of Jesus (chaps. 1–17; early third century); a Joseph source comprising Joseph's first-person experience of time suspension and Mary's postpartum inspection (chaps. 18–20; late second century); and a Zechariah source, which offers an account of Zechariah's death (chaps. 21–24; second century).[83]

Von Harnack's source theory was convincing and left unchallenged for some time until the discovery of the Bodmer Miscellaneous Codex in the mid-twentieth century, which proved that the text comprised all three sections (minus the "suspension of time" passage of chapter 18) at a very early date.[84] More recent trends too have seen a shift away from multiple source theories and have argued instead for the literary unity of the text. Hock notes that many of the discrepancies observed about the *Protevangelium* could be explained persuasively as various oral traditions available to the author as well as arguments dependent upon rhetorical reasoning.[85] Specifically, Bovon has argued that the switch from third to first person supports the overall goals of the text and makes even more emphatic the importance of the moment being described, namely the birth of Jesus.[86] Perhaps the strongest and initial catalyst for the shifting trend can be attributed to de Strycker and Elliott who argue that the vocabulary and compositional structure of the text point clearly to

83. Von Harnack, *Geschichte der altchristlichen Literatur*, 1:600–603. See also, Ehrman and Pleše, *Apocrypha Gospels*, 33 and Vanden Eykel, *Looking Up*, 23–26.

84. See section on Textual History for discussion on the absence of Joseph's first person narration in the Bodmer Miscellaneous Codex.

85. Hock, *Infancy Gospels*, 14.

86. Bovon, "Suspension of Time," 395.

a unified work.[87] Hock too observes the consistency of the text's syntax and word choice as evidence for literary unity, but makes the argument for concordance from a different perspective. Looking to the dominant theme of purity as the binding agent, Hock writes that "it is difficult to imagine anyone more pure than Mary" and that it is this overarching concern for her purity that informs the *Protevangelium* thematically and structurally.[88]

No new or substantial arguments have been made to shift discussion away from the current consensus that the *Protevangelium* is a unified text. In fact, various recent studies on the *Protevangelium* have presumed the text is coherent and such unity is used as a springboard or justification for other inquiries into the text, especially ones that employ literary analysis.[89] Important to note, however, is that the arguments for literary unity in the text do not exclude the use of sources by the author or the editing of the narrative at a later date. The author shows clear signs of literary influence from a number of different sources; the literary unity of the text simply holds the position that the *Protevangelium* can be read as a coherent whole.

Mary's Characterization as Virginal and Pure

Even the most cursory reading of the *Protevangelium* will reveal the deep and overarching theme of Mary's extreme and unparalleled purity. As a narrative devoted to providing more information about the mother of Jesus, every aspect of Mary's character is defined by her purity and every detail disclosed is for the purpose of enhancing her status. Perhaps most obviously, Mary's perpetual virginity dominates most discussions regarding her purity and has often been used as justification for viewing her as the New Eve, since she alone is immune to the curse placed on the primordial woman of Genesis (Gen 2:16) because of her extraordinary virginity.[90] No doubt, Mary is emphatically declared to be a virgin before,

87. De Strycker, *La forme la plus ancienne*, 6–13; and Elliott, *Apocryphal New Testament*, 50.

88. Hock, *Infancy Gospels*, 14–15.

89. E.g., Gaventa, *Mary*; Foskett, *Virgin Conceived*; Vuong, *Gender and Purity*; Vanden Eykel, *Looking Up*.

90. Although the *Protevangelium* does not explicitly compare Mary with Eve, there are parallels that juxtapose these two women. Mary's virginal and painless birth recalls the curse of Eve and all her female descendants and Joseph's evoking of the Adam story

during, and after the birth of Jesus. This claim is not simply vocalized by various characters throughout the narrative, but actually imbedded in her title as the Virgin of the Lord, an honor bestowed upon her the moment she leaves the sacred space of the Jerusalem temple (9:7). Every scene in the *Protevangelium* is carefully constructed either to ensure that her sexual purity is safeguarded or to verify that it is still intact.

Three specific scenarios in particular stand out as tests and proof of Mary's virginal state.[91] The first occurs when she is questioned harshly by Joseph about her pregnant state after he has been away for several months wherein he implies Mary was deceived and corrupted in a manner liken to Eve (13:1–7). Mary speaks only eight times throughout the entire narrative so it is especially significant that three of these occurrences involve defenses of her purity and innocence.[92] The first two of these three declarations occur when she responds to Joseph in a clear and active voice that she is innocent and has not had sexual relations with any man (13:8) and when Mary vows that she does not know how she became pregnant (13:10).

The second time Mary defends her virginity she does so in language similar to her response to Joseph, but the claim this time is made before the high priest: "I am pure before him and I do not know a man" (15:13). Mary's third declaration of innocence is also found in a tense situation involving the verification of her virginal state. In this second scenario the stakes are higher, but so are the rewards. When both Mary and Joseph are questioned about her pregnant state, Mary's virginal status is doubly defended not only by her own voice, but also by Joseph, who declares that he is pure concerning Mary. The testing escalates when the high priest requires them to take the "Lord's drink test" (16:3–8) with the purpose of disclosing their sin, moving the defense of Mary's virginity from a vocal declaration and a private affair to a physical testing and a public matter.

The third scene emphasizing Mary's sexually pure state and role as the Lord's virgin has the goal of presenting Mary as a virgin to an even

encourages a comparison between Mary and Eve. Moreover, when Joseph questions Mary over her state, it is precisely the same question God poses to Eve (13:6 cf. Gen 2:13). Among patristic writers, Justin Martyr is the first to make an explicit allusion to the Mary-Eve typology (*Dial.* 100). Irenaeus (*Haer.* 22) and Tertullian (*Carn. Chr.* 17) also draw allusions developed by Justin by focusing on Mary's obedience and proper belief. See Beattie, "Mary in Patristic Theology," 77, 80, 86–90.

91. For further discussion on these three scenes, see Vuong, *Gender and Purity*, 171–90.

92. Vuong, *Gender and Purity*, esp. 174–75.

higher level when she is questioned and given a gynecological examination by a midwife (20:1–2). The results, of course, are that the midwife physically confirms her extraordinary and paradoxical state as virgin mother (20:3–4, 10–11). In other words, Mary's pre- and post-partum virgin status is repeatedly established by all major characters in the narrative (Joseph, Mary, the priests, all the people, the angel, and the Lord God) and verified through the physical testing of both Mary and Joseph.

Additionally, Mary's perpetual virginity is addressed at several points throughout the narrative. Despite the author's decision to end the narrative shortly after Herod's wrath, various hints encourage the reader to expect that Mary's virginity remains eternally intact until the end of her days. Descriptions surrounding Mary's relationship with Joseph provide the most important clues. When Mary must leave the temple precinct, Joseph is chosen by lot to care for her (9:7). His hesitation to take on this role reveals the intentions of this marriage; namely, Joseph protests and calls upon his old age and children from his previous marriage as excuses for not taking on Mary as his wife (9:8). Also significant is the fact that the moment Joseph brings Mary to his home, he immediately disappears, offering no space or time in which his intentions towards Mary can be questioned (9:11–12). The so-called marriage of Mary and Joseph is dispelled in various ways to encourage the reading that this is no ordinary marriage, and that Joseph functions merely as a guardian rather than a traditional husband with traditional conjugal rights.[93] Joseph even refers to Mary as the Lord's virgin and is instructed specifically by the priests to "care and protect" her (9:7). The irregularities of their "betrothal" or "marriage" (no scene details an actual marriage ceremony) are again highlighted when Joseph is questioned by the midwife on the conditions of his relationship with Mary (19:1–11). His cumbersome and vague description ("I received her by lot as my wife. But she is not my wife" 19:8) reinforce that Mary's relationship with Joseph remains uncompromised even post-childbirth.

While Mary's virginity no doubt dominates her depiction as pure, scholars across the board have commented that Mary's purity cannot be so narrowly defined by her virginity. Reinforcing this view, Peter Brown describes the *Protevangelium*'s depiction of Mary as a "human creature

---

93. Cf. betrothal expectations and customs found in the Hebrew Bible as discussed by Satlow (*Jewish Marriages*, 69) to reinforce the oddity of Mary's and Joseph's betrothal or "marriage."

totally enclosed in sacred space"[94] and Beverly Gaventa has encouraged the term "sacred purity"[95] as a way to describe more accurately the overwhelming and diverse ways Mary's purity is constructed, discussed, and occupied in the narrative space of the *Protevangelium*. Indeed, the theme of purity dominates the entire storyline and is central to its structure.[96]

For example, ritual purity in particular plays a prominent role in contributing to the depiction of Mary as pure as demonstrated especially by the acts of her parents during her miraculous conception[97] as well as her birth and early childhood years. Simply put, ritual impurity refers to a state one enters as a result of defilements that can be contracted by having direct or indirect contact with various natural sources as outlined by the Hebrew Bible (especially Leviticus and Numbers).[98] Examples of such natural sources include childbirth (Lev 12:1–8), scale disease (Lev 13:1—14:32), bodily discharges like semen and menstrual blood (Lev 15:1–33), and human corpses (Num 19:10–22), as well as the remains of certain animals (Lev 11:1–47). Since such impurity can be contracted by normal, unavoidable, and even desired activities like childbirth, to be ritually impure is neither prohibited nor sinful and is a state that can be reversed by means of certain formal acts of purification.[99] The *Protevangelium*'s intention to present Mary as ritually pure appears at the

---

94. Brown, *Body and Society*, 273.

95. Gaventa, *Mary*, 109–10.

96. See esp. Vuong, *Gender and Purity*, 60–192.

97. Note that it is Mary's miraculous conception not her immaculate conception. Dogmatically defined in 1854 by Pope Pius IX, Immaculate Conception refers specifically to the Roman Catholic doctrine that holds that Mary was conceived in her mother's womb without Original Sin. Since the idea of Original Sin does not enter into theological debate until Augustine (354–430), it is anachronistic to suggest that the *Protevangelium* promoted this view. Rather, what is promoted is the idea that Mary was miraculously conceived.

98. Foundational contributions on the defiling systems outlined in the Hebrew Bible have been made especially by David Hoffman, Mary Douglas, Jacob Neusner, and Jacob Milgrom. Jonathan Klawans's more recent study on the topic (*Impurity and Sin*, 4–20) offers clear and concise descriptions of ritual purity and builds on the aforementioned contemporary studies on this critical concept.

99. By contrast, moral impurity arises from immoral acts and sins and is a severe type of impurity. Given that it is an avoidable impurity, it is often long lasting and cannot be reversed by simply participating in various acts of ritual purification. Only punishment and atonement are possible remedies for moral impurities and they serve only to lessen the impurity rather than completely wipe it clean. See further Klawans, *Impurity and Sin*, 24–26; and Klawans, *Purity, Sacrifice, and the Temple*, 53–56.

outset with the introduction of Mary's parents who pay careful heed to ritual purity laws associated with the Jerusalem temple. As righteous and pious Jews, they are faithful participants of the temple cult and are described offering more than the required sacrifices according to the laws and customs of their community (1:1–3). Mary's mother even dismisses her handmaid's offer of a headband that may have the ability to help her barren state (2:4). Whether Anna would have contracted ritual impurity from the headband is unclear, but the possibility of it is taken off the table when she does not hesitate to reject it, despite desperately wanting to conceive (2:5). Anna's and Joachim's conscious efforts to be ritually pure in the eyes of God are prominent ways their righteousness and piety are articulated in the narrative.

Perhaps the most obvious interest in ritual purity comes with Mary's birth when Anna intentionally refrains from breastfeeding her newborn child for fear Mary might contract the ritual impurity contracted by Anna through childbirth. Anna is said to have waited until the prescribed days were fulfilled before cleansing herself of the flow of blood and giving her breast to Mary (5:9). According to Leviticus 12:5, when a woman conceives and "bears a female child, she shall be unclean two weeks, as in her menstruation; her time of blood purification shall be sixty-six days." During this period of purification, Levitical legislation prevents such new mothers from entering the sanctuary and from touching any sacred thing until she returns to a state of ritual purity; it does not, however, prohibit the nursing of one's child during this period. Anna's decision to ensure an exceptional level of ritual purity by waiting to breastfeed only contributes further to Mary's superior purity.[100] It is not surprising that Anna continues to ensure all spaces and interactions with her daughter remain ritually pristine. After Mary takes her first seven steps, Anna vows that Mary will not walk on the ground again until she is taken up to the temple (6:3). This vow is almost immediately followed by Anna's decision to transform her daughter's bedroom into a sanctuary so nothing profane (κοινός) or unclean (ἀκάθαρτος) makes contact with Mary (6:4). The securing of Mary's pure state involves clean food but also companionship as only the "undefiled daughters of the Hebrews" are given permission to socialize with her (6:5).

As discussed earlier, ritual purity and impurity are the two states from which humans shift back and forth depending on their various daily

---

100. Vuong, *Gender and Purity*, 88–91.

interactions and activities. Why these states matter is wholly connected to the temple and the assumption of the efficacy of sacrifice to cleanse sins, as access to the temple is not possible in a state of ritual impurity. As mentioned above, the depiction of Mary's parents as utterly pious and righteous is fully articulated in terms of the temple and its protocols for ritual purity. Readers learn that despite having his gifts initially rejected (1:5), Joachim's first act after finding out his wife has finally conceived[101] is not to see Anna, but to gather his flocks in order to offer proper sacrifices. Joachim's gifts of ten lambs, twelve calves, and one hundred goats well exceed the requirements of any single offering (4:5–7); thus, Joachim's gifts are offered to atone not only for his sins and the sins of his family, but also for the whole community.

The text's concern for ritual purity as demonstrated via Mary's extreme upbringing suggest that Mary functions as a symbolic temple sacrifice (she is perfect, unblemished, and referred to as a gift to the Lord), albeit of a different sort—rather than dying on the altar, she dances on its steps.[102] Mary's stay at the Jerusalem temple has stirred much discussion over its meaning, but also as to whether it betrays a lack of knowledge of true Jewish practices since it features a woman living in the temple. A number of scholars have expressed this sentiment by comparing the *Protevangelium*'s description to what is known of Jewish traditions regarding the temple according to the Hebrew Bible and the Septuagint. Namely, the temple altar is restricted to the male priestly order and can only be entered at specific times and under specific conditions. Since Mary is neither male nor of the priestly line, her presence in such holy space has been questioned and used as evidence against the possibility of a Jewish author and/or Palestinian provenance.[103]

101. The Greek manuscripts vary on whether Anna conceived (perfect form) or will conceive (future form). The perfect form, which suggest Anna's conception of Mary was miraculous and achieved without intercourse (this is not an argument for Anna's virginity, only that the conception of her daughter was achieved without intercourse) is favored for the following reasons: 1. It is attested in our earliest manuscript; 2. The sequence of Joachim and Anna being positioned in two very different locations when the news arrives of the conception (e.g., the wilderness and garden) hardly seems coincidental; and 3. It is consistent with the goal of portraying Mary as exceptionally pure—Anna conceives miraculously in the absence of Joachim in the same way Mary will conceive miraculously in the absence of Joseph. On this position, see esp. Vuong, *Gender and Purity*, 166–70; so too, Shoemaker, *Mary in Early Christian Faith*, 56–57.

102. Vuong, *Gender and Purity*, 88–103.

103. Other details about the description of the sanctuary with regards to its lack of reference to the curtain and the Ark of the Covenant have also been questioned with

By contrast, Mary's stay in the temple has also been read as a con-tinuation of her exceptionally pure upbringing.[104] Anna's and Joachim's particular interest to keep her diet free from any defiling thing is further ensured when she is fed by the hands of a heavenly messenger (8:2) and the purity established by Mary's bedroom turned sanctuary is perfectly safeguarded in her residency at the actual Jerusalem temple and the holy of holies. While Mary is surely envisioned as a temple sacrifice of sorts, her remarkable purity has also convinced many that her body can be un-derstood as a temple itself and that there exists no more appropriate place for her to exist than the very holiest of spaces. She is, as Émile Amann describes, "already a consecrated spiritual creature. Her place . . . can only be within the holy of holies . . ."[105] In this way, the placing of Mary in the temple is interpreted as an intentional move on the part of the author to demonstrate concretely Mary's exceptional purity and ensure that it continues to be protected. Mary's purity is unparalleled by anyone and her ritual purity exceeds even those who are given permission to enter the holy of holies: the temple priests. Perhaps the author was wholly cog-nizant of the decision to break with temple traditions regarding purity temple practices in order to drive home his portrait of Mary as extraor-dinarily pure.[106]

However, the author includes one critical scene in which Mary's purity is questioned and it involves the reason she is temporarily forced to leave the temple. When Mary reaches the age of twelve, the temple priests begin to fear she might pollute the temple due to her impending menstruation. While it is possible to interpret this detail as a possible slight to women and Mary in particular, more nuanced readings look to reasons that are more congruent with the primary intentions and goals of the narrative. The author is aware that in order for Mary to fulfill her future role as the woman who brings forth the son of God she must first be acknowledged as able to bear children. Mary's menstruation, in other words, allows for her new role as the Virgin Mother. Indeed, her tempo-rary absence from the sacred space of the temple establishes her adher-ence to the proper laws for separation as outlined by Levitical legislations

---

regards to the author's ignorance of temple practices. See Vanden Eykel, *Looking Up*, 69.

104. Zervos, "Early Non-Canonical Annunciation," 690; Foskett, *Virgin Conceived*, 146–48; Vuong, *Gender and Purity*, 56.

105. Amann, *Protévangile*, 205. See also Vuong, *Gender and Purity*, esp. 243–44.

106. Vuong, *Gender and Purity*, 131. So too, Vanden Eykel, *Looking Up*, 69–70.

regarding menstrual separation. A disregard for such legislation is cause for condemnation, but menstruation itself is not.[107] Mary's departure from the temple does not taint her exceptionally pure status since she almost immediately returns to weave the temple curtains, after a symbolic adherence to the ritual laws.

The theme of purity dominates the goals, structure, and all plot points throughout the *Protevangelium*. While Mary's virginity is undeniably the more prominent concern of the text, there is clear interest in expanding the definition of purity in her case. The text's concern to present Mary as ritually as well as menstrually pure also shapes the ways in which Mary's purity is defined. Two other forms of purity also appear as interests in the text, but their impact is less significant. The first is "carnal impurity," a term coined by Christine Hayes to describe an extension of moral impurity, but is distinguishable from it because it relates specifically to the body and can be physically transmitted through sexual activity.[108] When Mary is being questioned about her pregnant condition, the accusations regard her sexual purity but also her carnal purity in that her innocence as well as her virginity are called into question and are being articulated in terms of sin. When Mary emphatically defends herself, it is a defense of both her sexual and carnal purity. The second of the two less prominent forms of purity is genealogical purity associated with one's lineage.[109] While subtle, the *Protevangelium* shows an interest in confirming Mary's genealogical purity as linked specifically with her Davidic lineage. Unlike the Gospels of Matthew and Luke who trace Jesus' lineage through his "adoptive" father Joseph, the *Protevangelium* is clear that Jesus *is born of a virgin*al woman who is a direct descendent of David.

The *Protevangelium* and Early Marian Art

Despite early theological discussions by major church fathers of Mary as the new Eve (see the section "Mary's Characterization as Virginal and Pure" above) and her highly blessed status as a model for purity and

107. Vuong, *Gender and Purity*, 129–33.

108. Hayes, *Gentile Impurities and Jewish Identities*, 4–16. Cf. Vuong, *Gender and Purity*, 156, 180–81.

109. Hayes, *Gentile Impurities and Jewish Identities*, 8–11, 58–59. Cf. Vuong, *Gender and Purity*, 169–70.

virginity, Mary is largely absent from early Christian art. As popular and widely disseminated as the *Protevangelium* was, even as early as the second century,[110] one would think that Marian pictorial art would be plentiful and aligned with the interest in filling in the gaps left by the canonical Gospels. In fact, early church communities often learned about biblical narratives, the apostles and saints, Jesus' passion, etc., not through books but from liturgies, sermons, and funerary decorations.[111] And yet, Mary seldom appears in the artistic imagination of early Christians before the fifth century. The few representations of her found in this period are often static profiles: Mary is frequently seated with Jesus in many of the third- and fourth-century catacomb paintings and sarcophagi.[112] While these images sometimes include animals like an ox or an ass,[113] there is little else that suggests borrowing of images from the *Protevangelium*.[114] The only exceptions are the sarcophagus from Le Puy at the Musée Crozatier with its depiction of Mary's and Joseph's betrothal and the sarcophagus of Adelphia from Syracuse depicting the Annunciation of Mary at the well (both fourth century). If the figure at the well in the third-century Dura-Europos painting is indeed Mary, these three depictions are the only testimony to the influence of the *Protevangelium* in early Marian iconography.

Mary was finally given a prominent position in Christian art in the fifth and sixth centuries as the result of major theological debate over her nature; many of the artistic works of the time drew from the *Protevangelium* as well as the *Protevangelium*'s literary descendants: Ps.-Mt.

110. Origen, *Comm. Matt.* 9.2; 17.1. See also the section above on date and transmission.

111. Cartlidge and Elliott, *Art and the Christian Apocrypha*, 15.

112. Jensen, "Apocryphal Mary," 291.

113. No ox or ass is mentioned in the canonical gospels. Origen's *Hom. Luc* .2:13–16 offer the earliest motif of ox and ass in the stable, but this motif becomes widespread around the seventh century probably because of *Ps.-Mt.* who described the adoration of the Christ child by the ox and ass; Nicklas, "Influence of Jewish Scriptures," 144. Cartlidge and Elliott also agree that the literary source for the ox and ass is *Ps.-Mt.*, but also cite the third-century sarcophagus lid fragment from Rome which depicts the nativity with an ox and ass to suggest that the motif is first witnessed by pictorial arts; Cartlidge and Elliott, *Art and the Christian Apocrypha*, 18.

114. Jensen argues that there are two paintings from the catacomb of Priscilla that are possibly the virgin and child and the Annunciation, but it is still highly debated, with some convinced that they are simply paintings of a mother and child since there is no clear indication of Marian style (e.g., water pitcher/source is absent); Jensen, "Apocryphal Mary," 292; Peppard, *World's Oldest Church*, 163–64.

and *Nat. Mary*. Rome's oldest and largest Marian church, the Basilica of Santa Maria Maggiore, for example, contains some of the earliest surviving artistic representations of the *Protevangelium* narrative. The Basilica was built under Pope Celestine I (422–432) and completed under his successor Sixtus III (432–440) shortly after the Council of Ephesus (431) in which Mary was officially given the status of *theotokos* (Bearer of God). Preserved solely in a medieval transcription, Sixtus's dedication for the main depiction of Mary seems to acknowledge her eternal virginity: before, during, and after (*in partu*) the birth of Jesus, thus drawing parallels to a *Protevangelium* tradition.[115] While the original image of Mary in this main depiction is no longer extant, the basilica's fifth-century triumphal arch mosaic and 43 nave panels are still largely undamaged.[116] Scholarship remains divided over the interpretation of the compositional scheme of the arch, but general consensus holds that the panel depicts various scenes from the life of Mary and her son as influenced by the *Protevangelium* and other apocryphal texts. For example, a majestic woman dressed in gold with a pearl diadem, necklace, and gem belt appears in one of the top panels between two buildings. Framing the overall scene, these two buildings position the woman with a skein of red yarn in her hand drawn from a basket at her feet, a detail indisputably from *Prot. Jas.* 10:7. Additionally, Mary's imperial garb has been interpreted as promoting her Davidic lineage and therefore royal descent.[117] No doubt Luke 1:27 con-

115. VIRGO MARIA TIBI XYSTVS NOVA TECTA DICAVI DIGNA SALVTIFERO MVNERA VENTRE TVO TV GENITRIX IGNARA VIRI TE DENIQUE FAETA VISCERIBVS SALVIS EDITA NOSTRA SALVS ECCE TVI TESTES VTERI SIBI PRAEMIA PORTANT SVB PEDIBVSQVE IACET PASSIO CVIQVE SVA FERRVM FLAMMA FERAE FLVVIVS SAEVVMQVE VENENVM TOT TAMEN HAS MORTES VNA CORONA MANET: "Virgin Mary, to you Sixtus dedicates a new dwelling; a worthy offering to your salvation-bearing womb. *You a mother, having born a child, yet having known no man, our salvation came forth from your intact womb.* Behold, the witnesses of your womb win crowns for themselves and each one's passion lies beneath his feet: sword, fire, wild beast, river, bitter poison. So many kinds of death, yet one crown endures." Text and translation from Jensen, "Apocryphal Mary," 289–90 (italics are mine).

116. Massive renovations of the basilica in the thirteenth century destroyed the apse and some later restorations have impacted the original images, but overall, they are in good condition. See Spain, "Restoration of the Sta. Maria Maggiore Mosaics," 325–28 and Jensen, "Apocryphal Mary," 289–90.

117. The identity of the woman is disputed. While most see her as an early Maria Regina because her clothing is consistent with the female garb worn by the imperial family, some have suggested other possibilities. Spain ("Promised Blessing," 518–40) argues that the woman is better identified as Abraham's wife and Isaac's mother, Sarah,

nects Mary to the house of David, but the *Protevangelium* is emphatic about this royal connection (10:2, 4). In the upper-right panel of the triumphal arch three figures in the middle are positioned in typical Roman marriage ceremony style; several scholars have suggested that this scene might depict the betrothal of Mary and Joseph from *Prot. Jas.* 9:1–11.[118] Finally, several scenes from the lower panels to the left of the arch depict Herod's massacre of the children with typical characters including the Magi; a women on the right of the scene appears to be escaping with her child. This may be Elizabeth, fleeing into the wilderness with her son John as in *Prot. Jas.* 22:5–9.

The images found at Santa Maria Maggiore are early and profound, but they represent only a partial picture of the influence of the *Protevangelium* on Marian art. Small ivory carvings dominate as the medium for *Protevangelium* inspired art well into the seventh century. Some of the more popular scenes in the carvings include the Annunciation to Mary, the bitter water test, Mary's presentation at the temple with the Temple Virgins, the miraculous birth of Mary, and Elizabeth's escape after Herod's decree. Perhaps the most popular scene is of Mary's Annunciation, which includes various details such as Mary at the spring or well, Mary spinning or with spinning tools, Mary with a pitcher or thread/yarn basket, and Mary with a rope and vessel. The position of Mary also varies: standing up, stooping down (to gather water), seated, face-to-face with the viewer, looking over her shoulder, and looking back.[119] Besides the sarcophagus of Adelphia mentioned above, several other well-known Annunciations include a fifth-century ivory book cover from Milan where Mary dons a dress and necklace while drawing water with her pitcher;[120] the sixth- to seventh-century ivories of the Grado Chair, where Mary is seen with a

---

because she is without a crown, *pendilia*, and red shoes—the markings of basic imperial regalia. Spain's proposal has been strongly criticized. See Jensen, "Apocryphal Mary," 301–3 who outlines the problems with Spain's Sarah theory.

118. Other possibilities include the betrothal of Christ or Joseph with the church as proposed by Schubert, "Die Kindheitsgeschichte Jesu," 81–89. General consensus among historians, however, is to view Luke 2:36 as the source; thus the scene is the presentation of Jesus at the temple with Simeon and Anna (see, e.g., Warland, "The Concept of Rome," 128–29).

119. See Peppard, *World's Oldest Church*, 165–79, for a detailed discussion of various Annunciation types.

120. Schiller, *Ikonographie der christlichen Kunst*, vol. 1, fig. 53; Peppard, *World's Oldest Church*, 166, fig. 5.3.

basket with spinning tools;[121] the sixth-century metal pilgrimage flask which displays Mary looking back from her work to see Gabriel;[122] and the ninth-century reliquary which shows a basket between Gabriel and Mary, though Mary is only holding her spinning tools, not actually doing work.[123]

Some of these Annunciation scenes are also part of a series or cycle depicting other parts of the *Protevangelium* story. Bishop Maximian of Ravenna's sixth-century throne attests to Mary spinning at the Annunciation, as well as Joseph at the bitter water test, a pregnant Mary riding on a donkey en route to Bethlehem, and the midwife seeking aid for an injured hand. The sixth-century ivory plaque (probably from Syria) now housed in the Louvre Museum in Paris features Mary spinning at the Annunciation on the far left of the image and Joseph at the bitter water test and Mary on a donkey as sequential images.[124] The ivory diptych of St. Lupicin from the same century depicts Anna's handmaid Juthine holding a headband, the item used both to tempt and mock Anna's infertility, positioned below another panel of the Annunciation with the Virgin doing wool-work, and a third panel on the other side depicts the bitter water trial and Mary conversing with Joseph on their journey to Bethlehem. The third example from this period is the ivory diptych housed at the State Hermitage Museum in St. Petersburg, which includes two scenes. The first is interpreted as the Annunciation of Mary's birth to Anna with elements of her lament as expressed by the nest of birds in the tree; the second is the mockery of Anna by her handmaid, Juthine, who presents Anna with a headband.[125]

By the fourteenth century, classical examples of iconographic cycles of the life of Mary with details from the *Protevangelium* appear ubiquitously in churches both in Eastern and Western Christendom. Cappella degli Scrovegni in Padua (Arena Chapel) stands as a classic example of the cycles of the Virgin that were appearing in the West. The chapel,

---

121. Evans and Ratliff, *Byzantium and Islam*, 47, no. 24H.

122. Peppard, *World's Oldest Church*, 167, fig. 5.4.

123. Peppard, *World's Oldest Church*, 171, fig. 5.9.

124. Jensen, "Apocryphal Mary," 295 fig. 16.4.

125. Cartlidge and Elliott, *Art and the Christian Apocrypha*, 38–39, fig. 2.10. Given the detail of the headband, Cartlidge's and Elliott's identification of the scene as the mockery of Juthine has been supported here over arguments that it depicts Mary's Annunciation of Jesus and Elizabeth's visit with Mary. See Jensen, "Apocryphal Mary," 293.

which was dedicated to the Virgin and its interiors designed by Giotto di Bondone, depicts an extensive life of the Virgin in twelve scenes starting with Mary's parents, Joachim and Anna, and the rejection of Joachim's gift at the temple because of his childlessness. Other scenes include Anna and Joachim at the gate, the birth of the Virgin, and a procession scene that has been interpreted either as the scene in which a procession of virgins guide Mary to the temple or when she is handed over to marriage.[126] In the East, the Kariye Camii (Church of the Holy Savior in Chora) in Istanbul offers an ideal example of the Eastern (Byzantine) cycle of the life of Mary. In this church, 18 scenes narrate Mary's famous story, including two separate Annunciation scenes of Anna and Joachim, Mary's first steps, Mary's stay in the temple where she is fed by an angel, and the choosing of her caretaker/suitor through the flowering of Joseph's staff.[127]

Pilgrimages, Piety, and *Protevangelium*-Inspired Marian Iconography

While the most majestic and grand pieces of Christian art can be found in cathedrals and churches via impressive mosaics and paintings on church walls, ceilings, and archways, art also played an important role in the expression of personal piety and devotion. Pilgrimages became incredibly popular in the fourth century and allowed for iconography to spread across the ancient Mediterranean world in the form of small, personal objects to be carried or worn on the body including ampullas, oil lamps, terracotta tokens or coins, and censers as well as rings and armbands. The most popular images were of the Cross and tomb,[128] but some of these souvenirs also depict fuller cycles of holy sites. Housed in the treasury of St. John's cathedral in Monza, for example, is a pewter flask that portrays various sacred scenes associated with holy places (the *loci sancti*). Mary features in three of the seven scenes: Annunciation, Nativity, and Ascension. In the Annunciation scene, Mary is spinning and looking back at Gabriel, again a feature whose literary source traces

126. Cartlidge and Elliott, *Art and the Christian Apocrypha*, 24, 26, fig. 2.4.

127. For a comparison of the two typical life cycles of Mary, see Lafontaine-Dosogne's exhaustive study (*Iconographie de l'enfance*), which also provides a list of every scene that has been depicted before the fifteenth century; Elliott and Cartlidge (*Art and the Christian Apocrypha*, 26) also chart out these differences based on Lafontaine-Dosogne's work.

128. Peppard, *World's Oldest Church*, 185.

back to the *Protevangelium*. From the Bobbio and Monza collections in Italy, approximately a hundred coins preserve images specifically from the *Protevangelium*. One noteworthy coin offers a unique scene of Elizabeth and John fleeing to the hill-country with Herod's soldiers in pursuit and an angel guiding them toward a mountain. In the Monza collection there is also a very early image of the Annunciation in which Mary is shown drawing water into her pitcher from a spring near a tree, while Gabriel appears above her. Encircling the coin is a blessing: "Blessing of the Mother of God, from the rock Boudiam(o?)."[129]

The *Protevangelium* is commemorated also at sites documented in early pilgrimage itineraries. Arculf, a Gallic pilgrim writing around 670, notes his visit to two churches that were built to commemorate Mary's Annunciation; current pilgrimages locate Mary's well at St. Gabriel's Orthodox Church in Nazareth.[130] The first church commemorates the spring by having water drawn up to the church from a spring and a well by way of a pulley system; the second church honors the house in which the angel Gabriel appeared and addressed Mary. In this way, the two-stage Annunciation scene in the *Protevangelium* (i.e., first at a water source and then in her home) transforms not only into a two-stop pilgrim site honoring the Virgin, but also into a recognized living and embodied religious act inspired by apocryphal imagination.

Observing the pilgrim Antoninus from Piacenza, Italy, Peppard writes that "this pilgrim [motivated by the hope of receiving blessings] used all of his senses, touching, and tasting more items in the Holy Land than anyone else did."[131] What Peppard's observation makes clear is that pilgrims, through their experience of visiting holy sites, were provided with an opportunity to have complex and multiple sensory encounters by engaging in touching, feeling, smelling, eating, hearing, and seeing the divine.[132] Pilgrimaging offered a powerful way to participate in religious devotion and personal piety. The *Protevangelium* iconography found on coins, flasks, rings, and armbands (items that were meant to be carried or on the body as amulets) as well as specific locales marked as sacred attests

129. Peppard (*World's Oldest Church*, 187) argues that while Boudiam or Boudiamo cannot be located, this coin represents one of the most locative of pilgrimage objects from the Holy Land because it names a specific place commemorating Mary's well.

130. Paulus Geyer, *Itinera Hierosolymitana*, 274 contains Arculf's description as reported by Adamnanus (2.24). See also, Peppard, *World's Oldest Church*, 189.

131. Peppard, *World's Oldest Church*, 188.

132. See Vikan, *Early Byzantine Pilgrimage Art*, 13.

to the narrative's vibrant influence not only on early Christian literature and art, but also on early Christian forms of religious practice, piety, and devotion.

Textual History, Transmission, and Translation

Presently no definitive edition considers all the textual witnesses and variants of the *Protevangelium*. While the third/fourth-century Bodmer Miscellaneous Codex is the most important witness for work on the original Greek text, its publication is part of a long line of editions and studies. After Postel reintroduced the text to the West with his 1552 Latin translation,[133] Michael Neander published a Greek edition of the text along with other apocrypha as an appendix to the Greco-Latin "Little Catechism" of Martin Luther in 1564 (republished in 1567).[134] The text appeared once again in a new edition by Johann Grynaeus in 1569 before falling into a long period of inactivity.[135]

In 1703, Johann Albert Fabricius's apocrypha collection brought the *Protevangelium* back to the scholarly limelight.[136] His contributions to the text's textual history involved initiating the first steps to a critical edition by providing both Neander's Greek text alongside Postel's Latin translation as well as his notes, annotations, and division of the text into twenty-five chapters (a second edition appeared in 1719). The *Protevangelium* appears one other time in Jeremiah Jones's 1726/1727 work (second edition in 1798), *Canonical Authority*. As indicated by the work's title, Jones printed an English translation of the *Protevangelium* alongside

---

133. Another Latin version was published a few years later in Johannes Heroldus's *Orthodoxographa*, 3–9, though it appears to be a significantly different translation. The precise identity of the manuscript used by Postel remains a mystery. Irena Backus ("Guillame Postel") uncovered a manuscript (London, British Library, Sloane 1411) written in Postel's own hand of his preliminary Latin translation along with a copy of the text in Greek, presumably from Postel's source, though it does not entirely match his translation. It is likely that Postel appealed to more than one manuscript.

134. This first Greek edition of the *Protevangelium* by Neander (*Catechesis Martini Lutheri*, 356–92) is based on an unnamed manuscript. De Strycker believed it to be Oxford, Bodleian Library, Arch. Selden B.53 ("Protévangile de Jacques," 340 n.2), though at the same time he says that Neander's text was "eclectic." Backus thinks it likely that Neander simply used Postel's Greek text from London, British Library, Sloane 1411 ("Guillaume Postel," 13).

135. Grynaeus, *Monumenta S. Patrum*, 71–84.

136. Fabricius, *Codex Apocryphus Novi Testamenti*, 1:66–125.

other apocrypha solely to verify the authority of the canonical gospels. Continuing this renewed interest in the text, Andreas Birch published an edition in 1804, which integrated two Vatican manuscripts (Vatican, Biblioteca Apostolica, Vat. gr. 455 and 654) into Neander's edition. New ground was broken with Johann Carl Thilo's 1832 apocrypha collection which included critical notes and commentary alongside a new edition based not on previous editions, but on seven new manuscripts from Paris, Venice, and the Vatican, of which Paris, Bibliothèque nationale de France, gr. 1454 (10th cent.) served as a base.

Constantin von Tischendorf published *Evangelia Apocrypha* in 1853 and a second edition in 1876. His 1876 edition would be considered the standard throughout the nineteenth and early twentieth centuries, remaining influential even today. For his critical edition of the *Protevangelium*, Tischendorf built upon the work of his predecessors and drew on a total of 18 manuscripts, eight of which were newly rediscovered in various European libraries.[137] His new text included a critical apparatus and added verse numbers to Thilo's division of chapters.

The discovery of the Bodmer Miscellaneous Codex in 1952 once again rekindled major interest in *Protevangelium* studies and began a necessary reevaluation of the text. Dating as early as the third or fourth century, the codex is a compendium of canonical and non-canonical texts: 1 and 2 Peter, Jude, Psalms 33–34, 3 *Corinthians*, the 11th *Ode of Solomon*, the *Apology of Phileas*, and *Peri Pascha* by Melito of Sardis. The portion containing the *Protevangelium* was published by Michel Testuz as *Papyrus Bodmer V* in 1958. In 1961, de Strycker's *La forme la plus ancienne du Protévangile de Jacques* drew upon the codex for the most complete critical edition of the *Protevangelium* since Tischendorf's 1876 edition. De Strycker's text uses the Bodmer Codex as a base text and compares its readings with various other manuscripts including those known to Tischendorf, but also later Latin, Georgian, Coptic, Armenian, and Ethiopic manuscripts. Significantly, in his investigation of the Greek tradition, de Strycker identifies 140 manuscripts, which he categorizes into five groups. De Strycker's edition has become the standard text though it is still provisional, as de Strycker admitted.[138] Perhaps one of the most striking features of the Bodmer Codex that contributes to its provisional status is its omission of Joseph's first person narration of the

---

137. Tischendorf, *Evangelia Apocrypha*, 1–49.
138. De Strycker, "Handschriften," 580.

suspension of time at the moment of Jesus' birth (chapter 18). Although brief, the passage poses textual difficulties since it is attested by a number of early and critical witnesses[139] leading de Strycker to conclude that it is unquestionably authentic ("La le personne est incontestablement authentique").[140] Convinced that this passage was part of the original text, de Strycker reconstructed the passage for his edition, thus supporting the idea that the Bodmer Codex, while our earliest witness to the *Protevangelium*, was still significantly edited and thus is not a pristine transmission of the second-century original text.

While most textual-critical studies of the *Protevangelium* have been spearheaded by European scholars, two major studies from North America, both in the form of PhD dissertations from Duke University, have made major contributions to the discussion. The first of these is Boyd Lee Daniels's "The Greek Manuscript Tradition of the Protevangelium Jacobi." After a succinct analysis of the text's place in history and its various versions and forms, Daniels catalogues in his three-volume dissertation, 138 Greek manuscripts known to him at the time (he did not have access to the Bodmer Miscellaneous Codex) and offers discussion and details for 81 of these. Completed in 1956, two years before Testuz's edition, Daniels's important work has received little attention, likely because it was overshadowed by the Bodmer discovery and was never formally published. In any case, it failed to reach a broad audience of scholars (e.g., de Strycker does not mention his work). Lamenting the lack of attention paid to Daniels's work, George Zervos used his own dissertation to collate the remaining 45 Greek manuscripts unexamined by Daniels. While several more monumental steps are needed to achieve the definitive critical edition imagined by Daniels and Zervos, their combined work has put this goal in reach of *Protevangelium* scholars.

A number of important English translations of the *Protevangelium* have appeared in the past few decades,[141] most of them dependent upon Tischendorf, some on de Strycker, and others on both. Some of the more

139. These sources, which include Florence PSI 1.6 (a fourth/fifth-century Greek papyrus from Turin), are listed in de Strycker, *La forme la plus ancienne*, 149.

140. De Strycker, *La forme la plus ancienne*, 149. Bovon was also persuaded of the passage's inclusion in the original text, but is more heavily concerned with other textual problems ("Suspension of Time," 395).

141. Other older English translations include: Hone, *Apocryphal New Testament*, 24–37; Cowper, *Apocryphal Gospels*, 1–26; Walker, *Apocryphal Gospels*, 1–15; James, *Apocryphal New Testament*, 38–49; Lightfoot, James, Swete, et al., *Excluded Books*, 27–48; and Cullmann, "Protevangelium of James" (1963).

popular translations include those by Cullmann, Elliott, Cameron, Ehrman and Pleše, and Hock.[142] While Elliott's and Cullmann's versions were used with frequency in the past, more recent and major studies on the *Protevangelium* have depended upon Hock's 1995 translation, with its revised versification system; the earlier verse divisions are provided in parentheses for ease of comparison with other editions and translations. The present volume follows in the footsteps of Hock's work by drawing primarily upon de Strycker's edition but in consultation with Tischendorf's edition. Of the other early papyri—P. Ashmolean inv. 9,[143] Florence PSI I 6, and Cairo JE 85643P—only P. Ashmolean has sufficient amount of text to be useful; readings from the manuscript can be found in the notes to the translation at chapters 13–15. When choosing another manuscript over de Strycker or Tischendorf, the choice has been motivated mainly for the ease of translation and to ensure the translation is accessible to a wider audience. Words added in parentheses restore material absent in the manuscripts or are added for clarity and consistency.

142. Cullmann, "Protevangelium of James" (1991); Elliott, *Apocryphal New Testament*, 48–67; Cameron, *Other Gospels*, 107–21 (a reprint of Cullmann 1963); Ehrman and Pleše, *Apocryphal Gospels*, 18–36; and Hock, *Infancy Gospels*, 1–81.

143. See Bingen, "Protévangile de Jacques, XIII–XV (P. Ashmolean inv. 9)," 210–14; all three papyri are presented in Wayment, *Text of the New Testament Apocrypha*, 73–79.

The Protevangelium of James

1 (1) ¹In the Histories^A of the Twelve Tribes of Israel,^B there was a very wealthy man named Joachim.^C ²And he used to double the gifts^D he offered to the Lord, ³saying to himself, "One portion from my abundance^E will be for all the people; the other portion for forgiveness will be for the Lord God as my sin-offering."

A. *Histories:* whether this account can be deemed an "infancy narrative" is challenged from the onset with the self-designation of "historia." Given that the criteria for infancy gospels (e.g., a focus on Jesus' birth and nativity) are not met in the *Protevangelium*, a sacred narrative about Mary may be a more apt generic designation. See section on "purpose" in Introduction.

B. *twelve tribes of Israel:* cf. 1:6 "twelve tribes of the people." This writing is unknown, but may be comparable to the *Book of Kings of Israel and Judah* (2 Chr 16:11; 24:27; 27:7; 32:32) or to the *Book of the Wars of YHWH* (Num 21:14) (Vanden Eykel, *Looking Up*, 106 n.18). The intentions of the reference are ambiguous and can easily be used to indicate a connection to the entire history of the OT (van Stempvoort, "Protevangelium Jacobi," 415–16), or simply an attempt at producing a family tree for Joachim and therefore Mary (Smid, *Protevangelium*, 25). *of Israel:* so Tischendorf and Syriac manuscripts but lacking in de Strycker (and P. Bodmer V).

c. *wealthy man named Joachim:* the name Joachim is likely influenced by Sus 4. Joakim, the husband of Susanna, is described as a rich man with a fine garden adjoining his house. Other references to the name Joachim appear in Neh 12:26 and Jdt 4:6 where Joiakim and Joakim, respectively, are identified as priests. While Joachim is not a priest in the *Protevangelium*, his level of concern for ritual purity resembles a priestly focus.

D. *double the gifts:* Joachim establishes himself from the start as a wealthy and devout man who goes beyond the requirements for purification and atonement. Cf. Job 1:5 who also presents extra offerings to atone for any unintentional sins that may be accrued by either himself or his family. Likewise, see 1 Sam 1:5 where Elkannah offers double portions for his wife Hannah.

E. *abundance:* περιουσίας, so de Strycker (from P. Bodmer V). Two-thirds of Tischendorf's manuscripts have this reading, though he favors περισσείας ("surplus").

(2) ⁴Now the great day of the Lord^A was approaching, and the children of Israel were offering their gifts. ⁵And Reubel^B stood up before him^C and said, "You are not permitted to offer your gifts first^D because you have not produced an offspring in Israel."^E

(3) ⁶And Joachim was very distressed and went to the Book of the Twelve Tribes of the people, saying to himself, "I am going to examine the Book of the Twelve Tribes of Israel to see if I alone have not produced an offspring in Israel." ⁷And he actively searched and found that all the righteous had raised children in Israel. ⁸And he remembered the patriarch Abraham because at the end of his days, the Lord God had given him a son, Isaac.^F

A. *great day of the Lord:* Cf. Joel 2:11; Acts 2:20; 1 Thess 5:2; and 2 Pet 3:10–13, where the phrase most likely refers to the day of judgement or related to the end of days, a possible usage here but with the caveat that it is also clearly associated with a celebration or festival. On its possible interpretation, see note on 2:2 below.

B. *Reubel:* Ῥουβήλ, so de Strycker. Many of Tischendorf's manuscripts have Ῥουβίμ ("Reubim").

C. *Reubel stood up before him:* while Reubel's position is not completely clear, his reprimand of Joachim has encouraged various readers to interpret him as having some authority at the temple. Indeed, several manuscripts include a description of him in the role of a priest. It is also very possible that Reubel is simply a busybody who has many children and wants to call Joachim out because of his childlessness.

D. *you are not permitted to offer your gifts first:* Joachim is not banned from offering gifts, but his childlessness prevents him the honor of doing so before all others. While there is no documented tradition concerning the order in which one may present gifts, likely he was able to lead previously because of his wealth and generosity.

E. *you have not produced an offspring in Israel:* childlessness in biblical literature was a common motif used to indicate God's anger and displeasure. However, in Joachim's and Anna's situation, this negative view seems not to be the case given the narrator's first description of Joachim as righteous. Instead, Joachim's and Anna's situation resembles the particulars of exceptional birth stories of matriarchs. Anna's infertility appears to be modeled after or at least reminiscent of Sarah (Gen 16–21), Rebecca (Gen 25:21), Rachel (Gen 30:1), Samson's mother (Judg 13), Hannah (1 Sam 1), and Michal (2 Sam 6:23). Even Elizabeth, Mary's cousin in Luke 1, is afflicted with fertility problems. That these important biblical matriarchs eventually are blessed by God and given children under miraculous conditions signals the expectation that Anna's fertility problems are not permanent and that she too will be able to conceive.

F. *he remembered the patriarch Abraham . . . had given him a son, Isaac:* cf. Gen 16–21. Joachim's remembrance of Abraham and Isaac encourages

(4) [9]And Joachim was grievous and did not appear to his wife, but sent himself into the wilderness and pitched his tent there. [10]And Joachim fasted for forty days and forty nights,[A] saying to himself, "I will not go down for food nor for drink, until the Lord my God visits me. My prayer will be my food and drink."   cf. John 4:34

2 (1) [1]Now his wife Anna[B] wailed twice over and spoke a twofold "lament: "I mourn my widowhood and I mourn my childlessness."[C]

the same expectation of Joachim's character as righteous and of a miraculous birth.

A. *into the wilderness . . . for forty days and forty nights:* cf. Noah and the flood in Gen 7:4, 12, 17; 8:6; Moses with God in Exod 24:18; Elijah's flight (1 Kgs 19:8); Jesus' temptation by Satan in the wilderness in Matt 4:2. See also Acts 1:3, when Jesus' ascension occurs 40 days after his resurrection. Note too that fasting and praying contribute to Joachim's righteous and pious character by evoking Jesus' stay in the wilderness (cf. John 4:34). The linguistic parallels between Jesus' 40 days and Joachim's 40 days are striking and evoke the theme of testing as well as death and resurrection.

B. *Anna:* Anna bears a common biblical name and her situation closely parallels Hannah's from 1 Samuel: both are infertile; they desperately pray and call upon God to help them with their barren states; and both are taunted and belittled by their slaves (2:6; 3:2–8; 1 Sam 1:6; 2:10). Like Hannah, Anna also uses song to express both her despair and joy, and their children, Samuel and Mary respectively, are dedicated to the Lord before they are born (4:2; 1 Sam 1:11). Additionally, Anna and Hannah wait until their children are weaned before leaving them at the temple (7:2; 1 Sam 1:22–23). Even the women's husbands share a noticeable closeness in their characterization and situation. Both Joachim and Elkannah, for instance, are depicted as pious Jews who go up regularly to offer sacrifices; Joachim is described offering double gifts akin to Elkannah's double portions offering for his wife, Hannah (1:2; 1 Sam 1:3–5). One final parallel is the misreading of the couples' situation by temple priests: Eli misinterprets Hannah's heartfelt and desperate prayer as drunkenness (1 Sam 1:13–14) and Reubel attributes Joachim's childlessness to his participation in sin (1:5). Other possible influences include Tob 1:20 where the name Anna is also used for the wife of Tobit and the prophetess in Luke 2:36–39, who is described as a widow who fasts and prays day and night, which is reminiscent of Anna's solemn prayer in the garden (3:1–8).

C. *I mourn my widowhood and I mourn my childlessness:* the despair Anna feels because of her "widowhood and childlessness" evokes LXX Isa 47:9 in which Babylon is punished for its mistreatment of Israel.

(2) ² Now the great day of the Lordᴬ drew near ³and Juthine,ᴮ her slave, said to her, "How long will you humble your soul? Look, the great day of the Lord is approaching, and you are not allowed to grieve. ⁴But take this headband,ᶜ which the mistress of the work gave me; I am not allowed to wear it because I am yourᴰ slave and it has a royal insignia."ᴱ (3) ⁵And Anna said, "Away from me! I will never do these things. The Lord God has greatly humbled me. Who knows if a wicked-doer has given this to you, and you have come to make me share in your sin."ᶠ ⁶And her slave Juthine

A. *great day of the Lord*: this specific day is referenced three times at *Prot. Jas.* 1:4; 2:2; and here at 2:3. Given its festive description, the Feast of Tabernacles has been suggested because "the last day" is referred to as "the great day" in John 7:37. Another possibility is Yom Kippur given the details of Anna's change of mourning clothes and the solemn but also celebratory nature of this holy day. If the latter proposal is indeed correct, the identification of the festival evokes a powerful symbolic connection between Jesus, the messiah who would bring final atonement, and his mother, the woman who was conceived on or near the Day of Atonement (Vuong, *Gender and Purity*, 75–79). On the view that Yom Kippur is both a day of solemnity and festivities, see e.g., Lev 25:10; *m. Yoma* 7.4; and Philo, *Spec.* 1.186–87.

B. *Juthine*: there are at least 18 variations with regard to the name of Anna's slave. De Strycker here uses Ἰουθίνη, but Εὐθίνη (P. Bodmer V), Ἡευθίνη, Ἰουθίνη, Ἰουθίν, Ἰουθήν, Ἰουθ, Οὐθίνη, Οὐθένη, etc. are also attested. Tischendorf has Ἰουδίθ (Judith).

C. *headband*: the precise meaning of the term κεφαλοδέσμιον is unclear, but given that it seems to be an item that is worn around or on the head, I have translated it as "headband." It is also possible it was more of a crown or diadem.

D. *I am your*: so de Strycker's εἰμὶ σή (P. Bodmer V); Tischendorf has simply εἰμί. The Armenian and Syriac fragments support the identity of Juthine as a slave belonging personally to Anna (from σοῦ εἰμί) rather than simply a household slave.

E. *royal insignia*: Anna's rejection of the "headband" may relate to the fact that it bears a "royal mark or insignia" and thus it may also be an indication of Anna's Davidic lineage, which is hinted at throughout the text. In the Armenian versions, Anna's royal lineage is made clear: "It is improper for me to speak with you like this, for I am your maidservant and you of royal character" (2.2; Terian, *Armenian Gospel*, 151).

F. *share in your sin*: despite the obscurity of the meaning behind the "headband," Anna's strong negative response to it reinforces the idea that the object may carry some form of transferable sin, curse, or trickery. Her rejection also emphasizes Anna's piety and loyalty to God since she will not participate in any questionable activity seen as contrary to God even if doing so might help her in what she most desperately desires.

said, "Why would I curse you? Because you have not listened to me? The Lord God has closed your womb^A to prevent you from bearing fruit in Israel."^B

(4) ⁷And Anna was very distressed. She took off her mourning clothes,^C washed her face,^D and put on her bridal clothes.^E ⁸And in the middle of the afternoon,^F she went down to her garden to take a walk. She saw a laurel tree and sat underneath it.⁹ And after resting a little^G she prayed to the Master, saying, "O God of my fathers,^H bless me and hear my prayer, just as you blessed our mother Sarah^I and gave her a son, Isaac."^J

cf. Gen 21:1–3

A. *closed your womb*: the term used here is ἀποκλείω; cf. the use of συγκλείω to describe both Sarah's and Hannah's infertile condition (LXX Gen 20:18 and LXX 1 Sam 1:6).

B. *Juthine . . . bearing fruit in Israel* (2:3–6): the interplay between Anna and her slave Juthine is reminiscent of the relationship between two other biblical matriarchs and their slaves: Sarah is mocked by Hagar for her infertility (Gen 16:4–5) and Penninah irritates Hannah for her closed womb (1 Sam 1:6). More specifically, Juthine's reproach of Anna parallels Reubel's rebuke of Joachim only a chapter earlier.

C. *mourning clothes*: Anna wears the mourning clothes of a widow who believes her husband is dead. See Esth 4:1, 3; Job 2:8; Dan 9:3, Matt 11:21, etc. for similar expressions of grief.

D. *face*: κεφαλήν, literally her "head."

E. *bridal clothes*: the rationale behind Anna's decision to exchange her mourning clothes for her bridal gown for the upcoming festival is difficult to determine with precision. However, if the festival is in fact the Day of Atonement, a tradition attributed to R. Simeon b. Gamaliel in *m. Ta'an.* 4.8 that describes the daughters of Jerusalem dressed in white and dancing in the vineyards on Yom Kippur, offers possible insight into this practice and its function in the narrative. The donning of white clothes also has clear eschatological overtones as seen in Rev 3:4–5 with references to the "day of the Lord" in Rev 16:15 and Matt 22:12.

F. *middle of the afternoon*: literally "about the ninth hour," thus about 3 pm. Cf. Acts 3:1 that also identifies three o'clock in the afternoon as an hour of prayer.

G. *after resting a little*: μετὰ τὸ ἀναπαύσασθαι, literally "stopping." So de Strycker (from P. Bodmer V), lacking in Tischendorf.

H. *O God of my fathers*: πατέρων μου, so de Strycker (P. Bodmer V lacks μου). Tischendorf has παρτέρων ἡμῶν ("God of our fathers").

I. *our mother Sarah*: τὴν μητέρα Σάραν, so de Strycker (from P. Bodmer V). Tischendorf has τὴν μήτραν Σάρρας ("the womb of Sarah").

J. *gave her a son, Isaac*: Anna's remembrance of Sarah's blessing (Gen 17:16) parallels Joachim's remembrance of Abraham at 1:8.

3 (1) ¹And Anna looked up towards heaven and saw a nest of sparrows in the laurel tree. ²And straightaway Anna lamented to herself, saying, "Woe is me. Who gave birth to me? What kind of womb bore me?ᴬ ³For I was born as a curse before the children of Israel. And I was reproached and they mocked and banishedᴮ me from the temple of the Lord my God.

(2) ⁴"Woe is me! What am I like?ᶜ I am not like the birds of the sky because even the birds of the sky reproduce before you, O Lord.

⁵"Woe is me! What am I like? I am not like the unreasoning beasts because even the unreasoning beasts reproduce before you, O Lord.ᴰ

⁶"Woe is me! What am I like? I am not like the wild animals of the earth because even the wild animals of the earth reproduce before you, O Lord.

(3) ⁷"Woe is me! What am I like? I am not like these waters because even these waters are calm yet leap, and their fish bless you,ᴱ O Lord.

⁸"Woe is me! What am I like? I am not like this earth because even this earth produces its fruit in its season and blesses you, O Lord."

A. *Woe is me . . . What kind of womb bore me?*: Anna's lament starts with the questioning of her own birth, which she describes as being cursed. Consistent with the biblical motif that associates barrenness with the unblessed, Anna sees her condition as wholly in the hands of God. Anna's lament, which surveys the procreation abilities of birds, animals, water, and earth, functions on several levels. First, it reinforces Anna's intense grief for being singled out, but also highlights God's creative power and a divinely created world that views motherhood and childbirth as part of the natural order.

B. *banished*: ἐξώρισαν; later Greek and Armenian manuscripts have ἐξέβαλλον ("thrown out").

C. *what am I like*: τίνι ὡμοιώθην ἐγώ; this phrase in each of the following verses has been translated in the active and present tense for effect.

D. *Woe is me! . . . O Lord*: this verse is lacking in Tischendorf. Other manuscripts combine the unreasoning and wild animals (vv. 5–6) into one stanza (see Daniels, *Manuscript Tradition*, 1:194–97).

E. *calm yet leap, and their fish bless you*: γαληνιῶντα καὶ σκιρτῶντα, καὶ οἱ ἰχθύες αὐτῶν σε εὐλογοῦσιν, so de Strycker (P. Bodmer V). Tischendorf (along with Armenian and Georgian manuscripts have γόνιμά εἰσιν ἐνώπιόν σου ("reproduce before you").

4 (1) ¹And behold an angel of the Lord^A appeared^B and said to her, "Anna, Anna, the Lord has heard your entreaty. You will conceive a child and give birth, and your offspring will be spoken of throughout the whole world."^C

²And Anna said, "As the Lord God lives,^D whether I give birth to a male or female child,^E I will offer it as a gift^F to the Lord God and it will serve him all the days of its life."^G

cf. Luke 1:31

cf. 1 Sam 1:11, 28; 2:11

A. *angel of the Lord*: the sudden appearance of an angel of the Lord recalls Luke 2:9 and Acts 12:7.

B. *appeared*: ἐπέστη is attested in most of Tischendorf's manuscripts and better suits the context. De Strycker (and P. Bodmer V) has ἔστη ("stand"); ἐφάνη (a synonym for "appeared") is also attested.

C. *your offspring will be spoken of throughout the whole world*: this phrase recalls Matt 24:14 and 26:13 where the words are spoken by Jesus with reference to the spreading of "good news." Cf. Rom 1:8 and 2 Cor 2:14.

D. *as the Lord God lives*: this phrase is commonly used throughout the *Protevangelium* to initiate vows or oaths (see Hannah's vow for her son Samuel; 1 Sam 1:11). It is also commonly used for the same purpose in the Hebrew Bible, e.g., Judg 8:19; Ruth 3:13; 1 Kgs 1:29, 2 Kgs 2:2; 2 Chr 18:13; Jer 4:2; Hos 4:15. While the vow Anna makes is presented here as hers alone, Joachim takes up his wife's words as a shared promise at *Prot. Jas.* 7:1. In the Armenian versions, the text inserts Joachim's voice in Anna's initial vow to make clear the promise is made on behalf of both parents (4:1; Terian, *Armenian Gospel*, 152).

E. *whether I give birth to a male or female child*: while Anna's prayer for a child and vow thematically recall other famous biblical tales of barren women who give birth to miraculous and special children, her declaration that she welcomes a child of either sex is noteworthy in presaging the birth of a daughter. All other significant births have resulted in male children (e.g., the sons of Sarah, Rebecca, Rachel, Samson's mother, Hannah, and Elizabeth).

F. *I will offer it as a gift*: Anna's immediate response to promise her child to God reinforces her righteousness and piety. By giving up her child as a "gift" to the temple, Anna promises to make a personal sacrifice to God. Additionally, her vow recalls other biblical children who are also dedicated by their parents to serve God. Specifically, Anna's declaration has parallels to the Nazirite vow that was open to both males and females and involved maintaining a heightened level of purity. Num 6:1–21 describes some of the requirements: being set apart for the Lord, abstention from the grapevine and all products produced from grapes including their seed and skin, and regulations on hair cutting. Samson (Judg 13:5), Samuel (1 Sam 1:11, 28; 2:11), and possibly even John the Baptist (Luke 1:15) all performed the Nazirite vow.

G. *all the days of its life*: Anna's vow for her unborn child is a life-long commitment; thus Mary's role as the Lord's virgin starts not on the day of her birth but the moment Anna utters the vow to the angel.

(2) ³And behold, two angels came, saying to her, "Look, your husband Joachim is coming with his flocks."ᴬ ⁴For an angel of the Lord had come down to Joachim and said, "Joachim, Joachim, the Lord God has heard your entreaty.ᴮ Go down from here; behold, your wife Anna has conceived a child.ᶜ

(3) ⁵Joachim went down straight away and called his shepherds, and said, "Bring me ten lambsᴰ here without spot or

A. *two angels came . . . flocks*: the message of Joachim's visit by an angel of the Lord by these two anonymous messengers (i.e., third-hand) reveals the excitement of this news among the people. The detail that Joachim is accompanied by his flock indicates his intention to offer immediate sacrifices for the blessing.

B. *Joachim, Joachim, the Lord God has heard your entreaty*: Joachim's response and return are joyous and celebratory—he immediately gathers his flocks to prepare offerings and embraces his wife at the gate. In contrast to Joachim's self-exile into the wilderness evoking images of death, his return is described in terms that evoke resurrection. Joachim's experience is described in language that foreshadows Jesus' own fate of death and resurrection just as the reference to forty days and forty nights without food or water resonates with the story of Noah and the Flood, which is typically interpreted as the death and resurrection of the world.

C. *Anna has conceived a child*: there is a discrepancy between the manuscripts over whether Joachim is told that Anna *has* conceived (εἴληφεν; perfect tense) or *will* conceive (λήψεται; future tense); de Strycker offers a good discussion on the manuscript variants on this phrase (*La forme la plus ancienne*, 80). The reference to Joachim "resting" upon his return at *Prot. Jas.* 4:10 has convinced some that the future tense should be preferred (e.g., Gaventa, *Mary*, 112). There are also a number of variations that attest to the future form. Textual evidence and narrative sequence, however, favor the perfect form, especially the idea that Mary was conceived miraculously and without sexual intercourse. The sequence of the announcements separately made to Anna and Joachim reinforce the geographical space between them and the idea that the conception happened in Joachim's absence—namely, Joachim is given the news of his wife's pregnancy before he returns from the wilderness (*Prot. Jas.* 4:3–4). Additionally, the idea that Mary was conceived without intercourse also aligns with the narrative's goal of depicting her as exceptionally pure. One further argument made for this reading is that the perfect tense is found in our earliest manuscript (Vuong, *Gender and Purity*, 166–70). While the preferred reading is that Anna conceived miraculously, it is not an argument for Anna's virginity; indeed, the narrative seems to indicate that she and Joachim had been trying for a child without success.

D. *ten lambs*: δέκα ἀμνάδες. Twelve lambs (δώδεκα ἀμνάδες) is also attested in some manuscripts.

blemish,^A and the ten lambs^B will be for the Lord God. ⁶And bring me twelve young calves, and the twelve calves^C will be for the priests and the council of elders. ⁷Also, one hundred male goats, and the one hundred male goats^D will be for all the people."^E

(4) ⁸And behold Joachim came with his flocks^F and Anna stood at the gate^G ⁹and saw Joachim coming with his flocks. Running straightaway to him, she hung around his neck and said, "Now I know that the Lord God has blessed me^H greatly. For behold, the widow is no longer a widow and I who am childless have conceived."^I

cf. Luke 15:20

¹⁰And Joachim rested^J the first day in his home.

A. *without spot or blemish*: cf. Exod 29:38 and Lev 12:6 on the regulations regarding proper sacrifices.

B. *ten lambs*: Tischendorf lacks the second reference to the ten lambs.

C. *twelve calves*: Tischendorf lacks the second reference to the twelve calves.

D. *one hundred male goats*: Tischendorf lacks the second reference to the hundred male goats.

E. *bring me ten lambs . . . for all the people* (4:5–7): Joachim's reaction to the angel's news of his wife's conception is striking. Rather than immediately attend to and rejoice with Anna, he first ensures that the proper offerings are made. His once-rejected double offerings are far exceeded by his magnanimous gifts of ten lambs, twelve calves, and a hundred goats to atone not only for his sins but for Israel as a whole.

F. *with his flocks*: μετὰ τῶν ποιμνίων αὐτοῦ, so de Strycker (from P. Bodmer V); lacking in Tischendorf.

G. *gate*: the close proximity to the gate and the reference to the temple situate Anna's and Joachim's home within Jerusalem.

H. *me*: με is attested in the majority of the Greek, Syriac, Armenian, and Georgian manuscripts and makes more sense in the context of Anna's announcement. De Strycker (from P. Bodmer V) has σε ("us").

I. *have conceived*: εἴληφα, so de Strycker (from P. Bodmer V). Tischendorf has the future λήψομαι ("will conceive"); and συλλήψομαι καὶ εἴληφα ("will conceive and have conceived") is also attested. See discussion in note on 4:4 above.

J. *Joachim rested*: the reference to Joachim's "rest" and its possible sexual connotation have convinced some that the discrepancy between whether Anna has conceived or will conceive at *Prot. Jas.* 4:3 should favor the future form (e.g., Smid, *Protevangelium Jacobi*, 41; Gaventa, *Mary*, 112, etc.). However, given the emphasis on purity, the chronology of the news, and that when the word "rested" is used at *Prot. Jas.* 15:2 in reference to Joseph and Mary there is no sexual ambiguity in its usage, it is likely that the intention is to present Mary as the product of a miraculous conception, thus emphasizing

5 (1) ¹On the next day he presented his gifts, saying to himself, "If the Lord God is merciful to me, the leafed panel of the priest's headdressᴬ will makeᴮ it clear to me." ²And Joachim presented his gifts and looked attentively at the priest's leafed headdressᶜ untilᴰ he went up to the altar of the Lord; and he saw no sin in himself.ᴱ

---

her purity by also highlighting her parent's purity by association.

A. *leafed panel of the priest's headdress*: the meaning behind πέταλον here is ambiguous (de Strycker, *La forme la plus ancienne*, 85 n.1). Literally translated as "the priest's leaf," the "leafed panel" appears to be connected to the priest's vestment and would have been made out of a kind of metal (perhaps gold?) that would allow for one's reflection to be seen since Joachim is required to look intently at it in order to determine his status. Exod 28:30–43 describes the vestments worn by the high priest, which included a breastplate and a band fastened onto one's forehead made of pure gold with an engraved rosette. The priest's "leaf panel" also has parallels to the headband offered to Anna by her slave; both seem to have possessed supernatural powers, albeit one positive because of its connection to the priesthood and temple, and the other negative as confirmed by Anna's rejection of it despite its possible ability to help her childless state.

B. *will make*: ποιήσει, so Tischendorf. De Strycker (from P. Bodmer V) has ποιῆσαι. Some later manuscripts have γενήσεται ("will become").

C. *priest's leafed headdress*: the leafed panel possibly also functioned as a mirror given Joachim's description of looking attentively at it in order for it to reveal his state through divine revelation as sinful or sinless (Hock, *Infancy Gospels*, 39 n. 5:1). The leaf panel may be a reference to the oracular power of Urim and Thummin as described in Exod 28:30 (1 Sam 14:41, 28:6; Num 27:21; Deut 33:8; Ezra 2:63. Cf. *m. Yoma* 7.5 where Urim and Thummin are described being embedded into the clothing). In Josephus's description of Urim and Thummin, these items were more stones than panels and they were positioned on the shoulder rather than forehead of the priest in order to determine the presence of God during sacrifices (Horner, *Jewish Aspects*, 319–20). Additionally, the more elaborate garments worn by the priest as described with the detail of the leafed panel, in contrast to the more simple linen clothes described in Lev 16:4, may indicate that Joachim's offerings are being made on a special day. The extra offering of gifts, the ornate clothing of the priest, and the references to the forgiveness of sins point to the observance of a special day, perhaps Yom Kippur (see note on 2:3 above on Anna's bridal gowns and reference to the great day of the Lord).

D. *until*: ἕως, so Tischendorf. Lacking in P. Bodmer V, likely due to scribal error. Some manuscripts have ὡς ("as if"), but ἕως is preferred since it is the more difficult and thus more likely original reading.

E. *no sin in himself*: ἐν ἑαυτῷ, so de Strycker and Tischendorf. Also attested is ἐν αὐτῷ ("in it"), which makes sense in light of the idea that the leafed headdress functioned as a mirror of sorts (see note on 5:2 above) and thus is the item that saw "no sin." My translation reflects the idea that the

³And Joachim said, "Now I know that the Lord God has been merciful to me and has stripped away all my sins." ⁴And he came down from the temple of the Lord having been justified and he went to his home.ᴬ

cf. Luke 18:14

(2) ⁵And her months were completed,ᴮ and in the seventh monthᶜ Anna gave birth.ᴰ ⁶And she said to the midwife, "To what did I give birth?" ⁷And the midwife said, "A girl." ⁸And Anna said, "My soul is made great this day."ᴱ And she laid her down. ⁹And

cf. Luke 1:46

---

sin is connected to Joachim even if it is reliant on the leafed headdress to confirm it.

A. *he came down from the temple . . . and he went to his home*: immediately following confirmation that Joachim is sinless and Israel as a whole cleansed by way of his generous offering, the text collapses almost all space and time before Anna gives birth, thus reaffirming Mary's most extraordinarily pure and holy status as she is born when all of Israel is free of sin and impurity. Joachim's offering and trust in the temple also articulates his belief in the efficacy of sacrifices for the cleansing of sins, as well as the way he and Anna demonstrate their piety in the narrative. See also Luke 18:14, which describes the parable of the tax collector who comes down from prayer at the temple to his home justified for being humble.

B. *her months were completed*: so Tischendorf and P. Bodmer V. De Strycker has μῆνες αὐτῇ ὡσεὶ ἕξ ("her sixth month was completed"). Other manuscripts attest to seven (ἑπτά) and nine (ἐννέα) months.

C. *seventh month*: τῷ δὲ ἑπτὰ μηνί, so P. Bodmer V (de Strycker has the synonymous ἑβδόμῳ). Tischendorf has ἐνάτῳ (ninth). The manuscripts differ on the length of Anna's pregnancy, including, six, eight, and nine months, but seven months is widely attested and is aligned with narrative tropes that depict divine or miraculous births. Thus it is likely to be the more original reading. In the ancient world, seven-month births indicated a significant event, a tradition that fits well with the narrative's characterization of Mary as exceptionally holy and pure. Other remarkable children said to have been born at seven months include Moses, Isaac, Samuel, and Jesus. Earlier editions of the *Protevangelium* favored a nine-month reading in order to be in accordance with biological reality, but the more difficult reading of a seven-month gestation is likely to be more primitive.

D. *Anna gave birth*: the *Protevangelium* here locates the birth of Mary in Jerusalem given their close proximity to the temple. Later traditions on the life of Mary also position Nazareth and Bethlehem as possible locales (*Nat. Mary* 8:5–6).

E. *my soul is made great this day*: the Feast of Mary's Nativity is one of the more popular festivals celebrated in her honor. Liturgies employed during the celebration were dependent upon the *Protevangelium*. Other feasts that drew from details in the *Protevangelium* include the Feast of Anna and Joachim, Mary's Conception and Nativity, the Presentation, and even Christmas.

cf. Lev 12:15

when the required days were completed, Anna cleansed herself of
the blood of her impurity,ᴬ and she gave her breast to the child,ᴮ
and named her Mary.

A. *Anna cleansed herself of the blood of her impurity:* τῆς ἀφέδρου αὐτῆς,
so de Strycker (P. Bodmer has the uncertain ἐφέγρου). Tischendorf omits.
Leviticus legislates that when a woman conceives and "bears a female child,
she shall be unclean two weeks, as in her menstruation; her blood purification shall be sixty-six days." Accordingly, ritual purity in the form of post-
partum pollution as well as its prescription is the concern here. While ritual
impurity is natural and not considered a sin according to the Levitical legislation, negligence in recognizing the state and responding with the necessary
purification rituals required to return to a state of purity, however, is cause
for concern. Anna's awareness of the impurities associated with the female
life-cycle, especially regarding fertility, indicates her pious character and her
acute knowledge of temple regulations, which state that while she remains in
the state of ritual uncleanliness, she may not touch anything considered holy
and may not enter into the sacred grounds of the temple.

B. *gave her breast to the child:* since there is no prohibition that prevents
a new mother from nursing her child even if she is in her period of purification, Anna's decision to wait until these required days were fulfilled before
breast feeding her child exceeds the necessary requirements of Levitical law
and thus is in line with the narrative's presentation of an extraordinarily
pure and holy Mary. Another possible interpretation for Anna's decision to
wait before nursing draws from Greco-Roman practices around early milk
(colostrum) and the general ancient belief that mother's milk was processed
uterine blood and therefore inadequately sanitized. Colostrum milk in particular was described as cheesy, difficult to digest, and the product of a new
mother's unstable body given its recent high discharge of blood (Glancy, *Corporeal Knowledge*, 111–12). If colostrum milk was indeed the concern here,
Mary's first feeding from her own mother would be a few days after birth
since colostrum in particular only lasts on average three to four days. While
this alternative suggestion is intriguing, the more natural reading seems to be
informed by the legislative rules regarding ritual impurity found in Leviticus,
especially given the narrative's deep concern with offering proper sacrifices
and keeping all laws regarding the temple. Despite being biologically impossible, this extended time prior to the commencement of Anna feeding her
child reinforces Mary's superior status and is consistent with the exceptional
life crafted for her by the text. A further interpretation is that Mary was simply wet-nursed during this time as was commonly done in wealthy families
in the ancient world, since death was inevitable for an unfed newborn. This
reading is surely possible, but given the text's emphasis on Mary's miraculous
nature, the intention may very likely be to indicate that she might survive
without food for such a long period of time.

6 (1) ¹The child grew stronger^A day by day. ²When she was six months old, her mother placed her on the ground to see if she could stand. She walked seven steps^B and went to her mother's lap. ³And her mother lifted her up and said, "As the Lord my God lives, you will not walk on this ground^C at all until I take you into the temple of the Lord. ⁴And she made a sanctuary in her bedroom and did not allow anything^D impure or profane to pass

cf. Luke 1:80; 2:40, 52

A. *the child grew stronger:* Mary's rapid growth exceeds the expectations of ordinary children and parallels the traits of remarkable offspring.

B. *she walked seven steps:* the ability to walk at six months contributes to the narrative's goal of characterizing Mary as exceptional. That Mary walks seven steps in particular draws again on her special status given the significant reference to the sacred number seven—e.g., the seven days of Creation. The number seven may also recall Ezek 40 with the reference to the seven steps that are described leading up to the new temple in Ezekiel's vision, especially given Mary's various connections to the temple itself: Anna's dedication of Mary to the temple, her upbringing and care by priests in the temple, Mary herself described as akin to a temple sacrifice, and then later on her status as a symbolic new temple.

C. *you will not walk on this ground:* while the policing of anything unclean coming into her contact with her daughter—even Mary's feet—is a practical impossibility, Anna's intentions are clear: to create an environment that encourages the preservation of a holy and pure child.

D. *anything:* πᾶν, so Tischendorf. De Strycker (and P. Bodmer V) omits.

through it.^A ^5And she summoned the undefiled daughters of the Hebrews^B and they distracted her.^C

(2) ^6When the child had her first birthday, Joachim made a great feast^D and invited the high priests,^E priests, scribes, coun-

cf. LXX Gen 21:8

cil of elders, and all the people of Israel. ^7And Joachim brought forth the child to the priests, and they blessed her, saying, "O God of our fathers, bless this child and give her a name that will be

cf. Luke 1:28, 30, 42, 48

eternally famous among all generations."^F ^8Then all the people

A. *impure or profane to pass through it*: the pairing of κοινός and ἀκάθαρτος recalls most notably Acts 10–11 where these two terms are used in the context of a debate regarding dietary restrictions and gentile impurity. Peter is told specifically in a dream that what was once deemed "profane and unclean" has been reversed by the Lord. The transformation of Mary's bedroom into a sanctuary indicates that this space is being guarded so that not only objects that pose a threat to her purity are eliminated, but also people and foods are strictly monitored. See de Strycker, who argues that the feminine pronoun "it" brings the concern for purity not only to the space of her bedroom but also directly to the body of Mary (*La forme la plus ancienne*, 91 n.3).

B. *undefiled daughters of the Hebrews*: Anna's interest in keeping Mary free from impurities extends to include monitoring her companions. Three criteria characterize those whom Anna will allow access to her daughter: they must be female, Hebrew, and undefiled. With regard to the third criterion, ἀμίαντος is often a term used to describe virgins or virginity (Wis 3:13; 8:20; Heb 13:4) or used in the context of ritual impurity (Wis 4:2; 2 Macc 14:36; 15:34; Heb 7:26; 1 Pet 1:4). The *Protevangelium* may be evoking both meanings in that Mary's playmates must meet the criteria of being female virgins, but also ritually pure.

C. *they distracted her*: διεπλάνων is here translated as "distract" in the sense of diversion. When the undefiled daughters of the Hebrews appear again at *Prot. Jas.* 7:4–6, they are summoned for a similar task: to distract Mary to ensure her purity continues to be safeguarded. Alternatively, see Hock (*Infancy Gospel*, 43 n. 6:5) who translates the word as "to amuse" noting that some manuscripts have διακονεῖν ("to serve/wait on"). Daniels has suggested "to wash" by offering an alternate yet similarly spelled word διαπλύνειν (*Manuscript Tradition*, 2:226–27).

D. *a great feast*: Joachim's announcement of a banquet in Mary's honor is almost identical to Abraham's announcement of a celebration marking the weaning of his son, Isaac.

E. *high priests*: τοὺς ἀρχιερεῖς, so de Strycker. Lacking in Tischendorf.

F. *they blessed her . . . all generations*: the banquet scene contrasts sharply with Reubel's reprimand of Joachim at the opening of the narrative. Both Joachim and Anna are welcomed not only by the priests, scribes, council elders, and all the people of Israel, but their daughter Mary is also given two blessings throughout the night. Whereas the blessing of Mary is repeated emphatically in the Gospel of Luke, this positive view of the priests is

said, "Let it be, Amen."[A] [9]And they brought her[B] forth to the high priests and they blessed her, saying, "O God of the Most High, look upon this child and bless her with an unending blessing,[C] which cannot be superseded."

(3) [10]Then her mother took her up to the bedroom-sanctuary and gave her breast to the child. [11]And Anna made a song to the Lord God, singing,[D] "I will sing a holy[E] song to the Lord my God because he has visited me and removed from me the reproach of my enemies.[F] [12]And the Lord my God has given me the fruit of his righteousness,[G] single but abundant before him. [13]Who will

cf. 1 Sam 2:1

inconsistent with the usual representation of Jewish leadership as manipulative and villainous found in the NT gospels. In addition, the priests' naming of the child during the blessing is odd given that Anna has already named her, but may speak to their position and role in her life. Mary will soon move to their temple to live and, inasmuch as the priests are her primary caretakers for this period in her life, she belongs to them just as much as she belongs to her parents. Hence their renaming is appropriate and highlights Mary's relationship to this holy space.

A. *Let it be, Amen:* the blessing is significant and represents the witnessing of Mary's honored and blessed status among the whole Jewish nation.

B. *and they brought her:* καὶ προσήνεγκον αὐτήν, so de Strycker. Tischendorf and P. Bodmer V have Joachim alone present (προσήνεγκεν) Mary to the high priest.

C. *bless her with an unending blessing:* this second of two blessings not only reemphasizes Mary's current holy status, but also suggests Mary's special future role as the mother of Jesus since the blessing is unending, extending over the rest of her days. Much like the previous blessing, this final temple blessing also emphasizes Mary as set apart by and for God. While Mary's infancy and early years are described in language that is resonant of a sacrificial gift—she is without spot or blemish (see Exod 29:38 and Lev 12:6; and note on 7:1)—the analogy is made complete with the double blessing bestowed upon her by the temple priests.

D. *song to the Lord God* (6:10–11): after Mary's double blessing, Anna responds in a manner that sharply contrasts with her lament in the garden. Anna nurses the child she so desperately wanted and sings once more, this time a song of praise filled with joy and happiness rather than sorrow.

E. *holy:* ἁγίαν, so de Strycker (and P. Bodmer V). Lacking in Tischendorf.

F. *reproach of my enemies:* the removal of reproach or disgrace experienced by Anna has parallels with the stories surrounding the birth of Hannah's son Samuel (1 Sam 2:1), but also Rachel's son Joseph (LXX Gen 30:23) and Elizabeth's son John (Luke 1:25).

G. *fruit of his righteousness:* righteousness is a term commonly associated with Abraham. Evoking the story of Abraham and his almost sacrificed son Isaac heightens the connection between the two miraculous children as well

cf. Gen 21:7 report to the sons of Reubel[A] that Anna is nursing?[B] Listen, listen, you twelve tribes of Israel: Anna is nursing (a child)." [14]And she put her down to rest in the bedroom-sanctuary and went out and served them. [15]When the feast was completed, they went down with cheer[C] and praised the God of Israel.[D]

7 (1) [1]Months passed for the child, but when she became two, Joachim said, "Let us take her up to the temple of the Lord[E] to cf. 1 Sam 1:21–28 fulfill the promise we made,[F] lest the Master will send some misfortune our way and our gift will be unacceptable."[G] [2]And Anna said, "Let us wait until she is three years old[H] so that she will not

---

as Mary's blessed status and symbolic depiction as a sacrificial offering.

A. *Reubel:* 'Ρουβήλ, so de Strycker. Tischendorf has 'Ρουβίμ.

B. *Anna is nursing:* the iconic depiction of Anna nursing her child makes clear that Anna's infertile state earlier was the result of an unfortunate circumstance that was made right with the divine will and act of God. The specific reference to Reubel highlights Anna's vindication from Reubel's harsh reprimand of Joachim regarding their barren state. See also the parallels to Sarah's celebratory words of being able to nurse her child, Isaac (Gen 21:7).

C. *cheer:* a few of Tischendorf's later manuscripts add: καὶ ἐπεθήκαν αὐτῇ ὄνομα Μαριὰμ διότι τὸ ὄνομα αὐτῆς οὐ μαρανθήσεται ("And they gave her the name Mary because her name will not pass away").

D. *praised the God of Israel:* the miraculous child of Anna and Joachim is thoroughly sanctioned by the will of God. This idea is reemphasized by the author's continued efforts to praise and thank God.

E. *temple of the Lord:* the temple features as the overarching theme in the narrative for the next three chapters, given the priests' concern with preparations for approaching, living in, and departing from the temple.

F. *promise we made:* Anna's promise made at *Prot. Jas.* 4:2 is adopted by Joachim. Cf. 1 Sam 1:21–28 when Elkannah, too, reminds Hannah of their promise and that their child is a gift from God.

G. *our gift will be unacceptable:* the description of Mary as a gift to God as a fulfillment of their promise reinforces Mary's symbolic status as a sacrificial offering. The same term (δῶρον) is used throughout the narrative to indicate sacrifices and offerings (see 1:2 and 5:1 as well as Anna's initial vow at 4:2).

H. *three years old:* cf. 1 Sam 1:22–23 where Hannah also waits until Samuel is weaned before sending him to the temple. Ages three and twelve mark two significant turning points specifically in the female life-cycle. *M. Nid.* in particular divides the female life-cycle into three parts (birth to age three; three to age twelve; twelve and beyond), whereby the ages three and twelve are especially marked as transitional ages. A girl's sexual vulnerability is said to be grossly heightened after three years and a day since she transitions from an infant to a minor (*ketennah*). Mishnaic understanding held that hymens could only be regenerated if she is younger than this age (see Horner, "Jewish

seek for her father and mother." ³And Joachim replied, "Let us wait."ᴬ

(2) ⁴When the child turned three, Joachim said, "Let us callᴮ the undefiled daughters of the Hebrewsᶜ ⁵and let them each take a torch and kindle it so that (the child)ᴰ will not turn backᴱ and

---

Aspects," 313–35).

A. *let us wait*: as mentioned above, Anna's decision to wait until Mary is three before she fulfills her promise parallels Hannah's promise. However, whereas Elkannah does not follow up to ensure his wife's oath is fulfilled and in fact recedes into the background of the narrative leaving Hannah as solely responsible for fulfilling her vow (1 Sam 1:23), Joachim takes on a more active role in his wife's promise. Joachim initiates the conversation of bringing Mary to the temple, transforming his wife's initial vow into a shared vow: "Let *us* take her up"; "the promise *we* made"; "*our* misfortune"; "*our* gift." Anna's response is also noticeably distinct from Hannah in that Hannah's reason is specifically related to weaning Samuel, whereas Anna's concern involves Mary missing both her mother and father. Joachim's dynamic role continues when he explicitly states that both he and Anna will be involved with ensuring Mary's safe arrival at the temple when arrangements are made to bring in "undefiled daughters of the Hebrews" to escort her to the temple.

B. *let us call*: καλέσωμεν, so de Strycker (from P. Bodmer V). Tischendorf has καλέσατε ("call").

C. *undefiled daughters of the Hebrews*: the precise identity of these daughters is obscured. Since they are described as a group, it is possible to interpret them as a group or "certain class," connected by their shared status as likely virgins (Smid, *Protevangelium Jacobi*, 51). It's possible, however, that their undefiled nature may also extend beyond simply their sexual purity to include other polluting factors including ritual impurity, since Anna strictly monitors those allowed to interact with her daughter to ensure Mary remains both sexually and ritually pure. While the "undefiled daughters of the Hebrews" is not clearly attested as a distinct group in either the HB, LXX, or NT, this group does share parallels with a group of women whose function seems to be the protection of the Egyptian virgin Aseneth in *Joseph and Aseneth* (Vanden Eykel, *Looking Up*, 74 n.27). There are, however, two instances in which similar phrasing is evoked: first, Judith refers to herself as the "daughter of the Hebrews" (Jdt 10:12) when she is being questioned about her identity by an Assyrian patrol en route to complete her mission; and second, Elizabeth (Luke 1:5) is described as being "from the daughters of Aaron." In both cases the description of the identity emphasizes ethnicity or lineage, but not virginal status and thus is distinct from the purpose evoked with the "undefiled daughters of the Hebrews" in the *Protevangelium* (see also note on 6:5).

D. *the child*: ἡ παῖς, so Tischendorf. Lacking in de Strycker and P. Bodmer V.

E. *will not turn back*: Mary's extraordinarily protected living arrangement in her home sanctuary continues even on her trip to live at the temple. The

have her heart captivated away from the temple of the Lord." [6]And they did this until they ascended to the temple of the Lord.[A] [7]And the priest accepted her, and kissed her, and blessed her[B] and said, "The Lord God[C] exalted your name among all the generations. [8]In you the Lord will reveal his redemption to the children of Israel at the end of days."

---

narrative leaves no space for the slightest challenge to Mary's pure state as she is guided by the undefiled daughters of the Hebrews.

A. *they ascended to the temple of the Lord:* the Presentation of the Blessed Virgin Mary commemorating Mary's entrance into the temple is celebrated on November 21 (Julian calendar: December 4). Considered one of the great feasts in the churches of both the East (from the eighth century) and West (eleventh century), this event is first attested in the *Protevangelium*. Her entrance and stay in the temple has often been interpreted in the liturgies of the East as preparation for her role as the mother of God—Mary is a temple in a temple. The Greek Orthodox *Festal Menaion*, for instance, makes this analogy (Vanden Eykel, *Looking Up*, 66–67).

B. *accepted her, and kissed her, and blessed her:* similar to the other blessings (6:7; 6:9), this third and final blessing continues to preclude possible questions regarding Mary's stay in the temple, while also highlighting her role as the mother of the messiah and therefore as an active participant in the redemption of Israel as a whole. Cf. *T. Levi* 18:1–11; *T. Benj.* 4:2 and 9:2; *T. Dan* 5:10; *T. Gad* 8:1, all of which express the view that Jesus would make salvation possible to the whole of Israel.

C. *the Lord God:* Κύριος ὁ Θεός, so de Strycker. Tischendorf has only Κύριος.

(3) ⁹And he set her down on the third step of the altarᴬ and
the Lord God cast grace upon her. ¹⁰And she danced on her feet,ᴮ
and the whole house of Israel loved her.ᶜ

8 (1) ¹And her parents went away marveling and praising and
glorifyingᴰ God the Master because their childᴱ did not look back

---

A. *third step of the altar:* traditionally only priests could approach the
temple in Jerusalem (cf. Lev 16:3–4, access restricted to the male priestly
Levite line; as daughter and non-priest from the Davidic line, Mary meets
none of these requirements). However, historical accuracy is not the point of
this detail; instead, it reflects the narrative's consistent goal of depicting Mary
as so naturally exceptional that readers would not be moved to question the
narrative but would expect the holiest of locales, even the steps of the altar
itself, to be her dwelling place. The third step in particular also has parallels
with the reference to the description of the third step of the altar in Ezek
43:13–17.

B. *she danced on her feet:* although Mary is depicted as her parents' offering (see note on 7:1 above), she clearly is no ordinary sacrifice in that she
dances rather than dies on the altar. The strict upbringing of her childhood
home where she is not allowed to touch the ground contrasts sharply with
the freedom she is given while living in the temple (Foskett, *Virgin Conceived*,
104–5). References to dancing in the HB and NT are often scattered and related to celebrations of thanksgiving (e.g., David dances before the Lord both
with men and alone upon bringing the Ark of the Covenant to Jerusalem;
2 Sam 5:6–16), but also as an expression of cultic worship (e.g., "Song of the
Sea"; Exod 15:1–18). The depiction of Mary dancing may be drawing on both
of these ideas: she celebrates her blessed role in salvation history, but also
her dance depicts her as a worshiper of God (Vanden Eykel, *Looking Up*, 86).

C. *the whole house of Israel loved her:* the last detail of this chapter reinforces the universal feeling directed towards Mary in her new home. Not only
is she accepted by the priests with their blessings and kissing, but Mary seems
to be content with her new living conditions, a position wholly embraced by
the nation of Israel. The approval of her stay is indicative of the expectation
that her new home, the sacred Jerusalem temple, will continue to safeguard
her purity.

D. *praising and glorifying:* ἐπαινοῦντες καὶ δοξάζοντες, so De Strycker and
P. Bodmer V. Tischendorf has only αἰνοῦντες "praising."

E. *the child:* ἡ παῖς, so Tischendorf. Lacking in de Strycker and P. Bodmer
V.

cf. 1 Kgs 19:5–8;
Ps 77:25 LXX;
Wis 16:20
at them.^A ^2Mary was in the temple of the Lord,^B nurtured like a dove,^C receiving her food from the hand of an angel.^D

A. *their child did not look back at them:* the fitness of Mary's new home is further reinforced when the narrator describes the comfort she experiences at the temple so much so that she does not look back at her parents. Anna's and Joachim's disappearance from the narrative from this point on also buttresses their role as initial protectors of Mary's purity and deliverers of their child to the temple. *at them:* ἐπ᾽ αὐτούς, so de Strycker (from P. Bodmer V). Tischendorf has εἰς τὰ ὀπίσω ("to the things behind [her]")

B. *Mary was in the temple of the Lord:* the text offers no real details about Mary's stay in the temple except the manner of her diet. *Prot. Jas.* 13:7 and 15:11 both emphasize, however, that Mary's childhood years in the temple took place specifically in the Holy of Holies. If this is in fact where Mary exclusively stayed, her first human contact would only come when the high priest enters into the Holy of Holies to pray about her at 8:5–6, since traditionally access to the Holy of Holies was permitted only once a year on Yom Kippur to offer sacrifice for atonement.

C. *nurtured like a dove:* the metaphor of Mary as a sacrificial gift is reinforced by likening her to a dove since doves were the only birds that could be sacrificially offered according to Pentateuchal law. The metaphor of the dove also evokes imagery from the NT Gospels, esp. the descent of the Holy Spirit (e.g., John 1:32; Mark 1:10; Luke 3:22) and the Spirit of God (e.g., Matt 3:16), but also as a symbol of innocence (Matt 10:16), peace, and purity—traits closely aligned with Mary. The image of the dove appears again, perhaps not coincidentally, as a sign by God used to determine the one worthy to guard Mary when it appears and lands on Joseph's rod (9:6). There may also be parallels between Mary's depiction as a dove with LXX Song 6:9 and even Philo's description of the high priests taking on a form that is neither human nor God when entering into the Holy of Holies (*Somn.* 2.189).

D. *food from the hand of an angel:* being fed by angels recalls the motif of "food of angels" (cf. Exod. 16:11–36; Wis 16:20–23) and the important biblical figures who are recipients of such heavenly nourishment. See 1 Kings 19:5–8 which describes Elijah who also receives food from an angel but also Wis 16:20; *T. Levi* 8:5; LXX Ps 77:24–25; *LAB* 19:5a; *5 Ezra* 1:17–19; *LAE* 4:2; Rev 2:17b; *Jos. Asen.* 16:14 for Jewish and Christian parallels. Whether Mary is being fed angelic food by the angel or simply regular food by an angel is unclear, but the manner in which she eats is clearly consistent with her extraordinary status. The narrative's decision to address Mary's very human need to eat, albeit by remarkable means, may also speak to the text's concern to present Mary in indisputably human terms. If the food is angelic, honey and honeycomb are described as being the food of the gods (e.g., Aseneth is brought a honeycomb by an angelic figure) as is manna from heaven (e.g., Moses is told by God that he will send down bread from heaven; Exod. 16). It is also probably not coincidental that the blessing Mary receives before the detail of her eating from the hand of an angel highlights her part in salvation history (cf. 7:4); thus the special diet supports her role in bringing redemption to the children of Israel.

(2) [3]But when she turned twelve,[A] the priests held a meeting and said, "Behold, Mary has become twelve years old in the temple of the Lord. [4]What should we do with her lest she defile the temple[B] of the Lord our God?"[C] [5]And they said to the high priest,[D] "You have stood upon the altar of the Lord; enter and pray

A. *twelve*: Mary's age of twelve indicates that her stay at the temple lasted nine years given her arrival at three years of age. The age of twelve is significant as it marks the transition from girlhood to womanhood in mishnaic writing (cf. note on 7:2 on the age three). In *m. Nid.* age twelve is specifically associated with puberty and is evidenced by the experience of menstruation, the implied reason why the priest here proposes she must leave the temple.

B. *lest she defile the temple*: while the narrative never states the issue of menstruation outright, the priests are clearly concerned with the potential pollution of the temple. Menstrual blood as the culprit pollutant rather than any broader pollutant associated with women is evidenced by the double reference to Mary's age of twelve years; use of the term μιαίνω to describe the defiling element (a word often used in connection with ritual impurity); and information from other early Jewish texts that attest to the prohibition of menstruant women in the temple. The *Temple Scroll*, for instance, indicates that menstruant women must be isolated during their impure period and prohibited from living in Jerusalem (e.g., 11Q19 48.13–17), while Josephus's description of menstruant women states they are restricted from the temple during this time (*B.J.* 5.5.6 [227]). Early Christian literature also dictates barring menstruants from sacred spaces. Luke 2:21–24, for instance, attests to Mary's access to the temple being restricted during the period of her postpartum impurity, and Hippolytus's *Trad. Ap.* 20.6 forbids baptism of female catechumens on the day they happen to be menstruating. Further, Dionysius of Alexandria's Epistle to Basilides (PG 10.1281–82), explains why menstruant women need to be refused church entrance, and the *Didascalia Apostolorum* (Vööbus, *Didascalia Apostolorum*, 244–45) attests to the abstention of prayer, the Eucharist, and Scripture by menstruant women, reinforcing in all three cases that the ritual impurity elicited from menstrual blood is viewed as highly incompatible with the sacredness of the church. This scene is designed to highlight the path Mary must follow to take up her consistently blessed position as the mother of Jesus, and adherence to laws regarding menstrual separation serve to heighten the depiction of Mary as pious and akin to priests who are always conscious of their ritually pure or impure states.

C. *Lord our God*: Κυρίου τοῦ Θεοῦ ἡμῶν, so de Strycker (from P. Bodmer V). Tischendorf has only Κυρίου.

D. *they said to the high priest*: καὶ εἶπον τῷ ἀρχιερεῖ, so Tischendorf. De Strycker (from P. Bodmer V) has the erroneous καὶ εἶπαν αὐτῷ οἱ ἱερεῖς ("the priests said to him"). That this specific priest must stand on the altar of the Lord and lead the other priests suggests he is not simply any priest, but the high priest.

concerning her, and we will do whatever the Lord God reveals to you."^A

(3) ⁶And the high priest^B entered and took (the garment with) the twelve bells^C into the Holy of Holies and he prayed about her. ⁷And behold, an angel of the Lord appeared^D and said to him, "Zechariah, Zechariah,^E go out and call together the widowers of the people and have each bring a rod;^F ⁸and she will become the wife^G of the one to whom the Lord God^H gives a sign."^I ⁹The

cf. Luke 1:5–23
cf. Num 17:1–9

A. *whatever the Lord God reveals to you:* with the office of the high priest comes special access to divine knowledge and interaction as depicted earlier with the confirmation of Joachim's sinlessness in 5:1–3, but also here when the priests leave Mary's fate up to God. Their position and special privilege is clearly sanctioned by God in that a response is received almost immediately once the prayer has been made.

B. *high priest:* so Tischendorf. De Strycker (from P. Bodmer V) again has "priest."

C. *garment with the twelve bells:* literally, "twelve bells," thus "garment" has been added for clarity. The twelve bells resonate with the references in Exod 28:33 and 39:25–26 as part of the priestly vestments. Specifically, the bells sit between blue, purple, and crimson yarn at the lower hem of the robe. The description of this garment is required by the high priest who must don the appropriate dress to enter the Holy of Holies when asking for divine help and intervention. Cf. 5:2, when another part of the high priest's garments (i.e., the metal panel on the headband) is used to elicit a response from God.

D. *appeared:* ἔστη (lit., "stood"), so de Strycker (from P. Bodmer V). Tischendorf has ἐπέστη ("appeared").

E. *Zechariah, Zechariah:* as in Luke, this Zechariah is also identified as a high priest with direct access to God and to angelic visits.

F. *rod:* see note on 9:8 below on the use of a cane instead of a rod in later translations.

G. *wife:* despite the use of the term here, there seems to be no support for the notion that Mary and Joseph participate in a relationship that is likened to a true marriage. Indeed, the priest at 9:4 will clarify that Joseph's role as it relates to Mary is simply of protection and guardianship. Cf. Matt and Luke in which Mary and Joseph are described as participating in abstinence before their marriage, but not necessarily after the birth of Jesus since Matt 1:25 notes that she remained this way "until she had borne a son." Whether Mary remained a virgin in her marriage is reasonably questionable given the references to Jesus' brothers and sisters at Mark 3:31–32, 6:3 par.; John 7:3–10; Gal 1:19.

H. *Lord God:* Κύριος ὁ Θεός, so de Strycker (from P. Bodmer V). Tischendorf has only Κύριος.

I. *Lord God gives a sign:* God's presence and control of the events that unfold in the narrative are illustrated through the answered prayers of worthy

heralds went forth to all the countryside of Judea. The trumpet of the Lord^A sounded and behold, everyone came running.

9 (1) ¹And Joseph threw down his carpenter's axe^B and went to their meeting. ²When they had gathered at the same place they went to the high priest^C taking their rods. ³After receiving all the rods,^D the high priest^E entered into the temple and prayed. ⁴When he finished his prayer, he took the rods and went outside and gave them back. ⁵But there was no sign on them. Joseph received the last rod ⁶and, behold, a dove came out of the rod and landed^F on

cf. Matt 1:18;
Luke 1:27

---

recipients as seen at 8:6 with the high priest's prayer and Anna's lament at 2:9, but they are also seen with the use of lots. The instruction for each widower to bring a rod sets up a scenario in which the rod has clear divining powers and is used as an indicator of God's will. Mary's fate is left wholly up to God's discretion. Cf. esp. Num 17:1–5; Hos. 4:12.

A. *trumpet of the Lord*: it is not clear which, if any, specific trumpet of the Lord is referred to here, but there are numerous biblical references to trumpets that indicate the presence of God (Exod. 19:16; 20:18); the praising of God (Ps 98:4–6, 150:3); the initiation of a feast or festival (Ps 81:3); the marking of an oath or an anointing (2 Chr 15:14; 1 Kgs 1:39); a celebratory event (1 Chr 13:8, 15:28); and for the purpose of gatherings and public announcements (Judg 3:27). 2 Chr 5:12–13 and Ezra 3:10 specifically indicate that the priests are the ones blowing the trumpets for the purpose of praising and glorifying God.

B. *Joseph threw down his carpenter's axe*: the introduction of Joseph here recalls Joseph from Luke and Matthew, though he is only (indirectly) identified as a carpenter in Matt 13:55. The depiction of Joseph here as a widower as well as his relationship with Mary, however, do not find resonances in the canonical Gospels. The *Protevangelium* makes clear that their "marriage" is not of the traditional type but one that resembles a parent/guardian and child relationship. While Luke 2:4 connects Joseph with the Davidic lineage, the *Protevangelium* repeatedly connects Jesus to the family of David maternally (i.e., via Mary).

C. *high priest*: so Tischendorf. De Strycker (from P. Bodmer V) again has "priest."

D. *rods*: that the rods themselves are instruments of divination used to carry out God's will is reinforced by the physical gathering of them by the high priest, their presence before God in the temple, and their being prayed upon in order to reveal God's will. The details of this scene reveal God's sanction of the priestly office and the temple as the appropriate locale for divine presence and prophecy.

E. *high priest*: de Strycker (following P. Bodmer V) has only "priest." Tischendorf has "he (entered)."

F. *landed*: ἐπεστάθη, so de Strycker (from P. Bodmer V). Tischendorf has

Joseph's head.[A] [7]And the high priest[B] said, "Joseph, Joseph,[C] you have been chosen by lot to receive the virgin of the Lord[D] into your guardianship."[E]

ἐπετάσθη ("flew").

A. *a dove . . . landed on Joseph's head:* cf. Num 17:1–9 in which a similar rod is used to determine the legitimate priestly line, which would thus be responsible for caring for the temple. Earlier, Mary's upbringing is described in language reminiscent of a temple sacrifice (see note on 7:1); here she is now depicted as a temple herself by way of Joseph being chosen to guard her. Not coincidentally, the metaphor of Mary as temple coincides precisely with the moment the priests are trying to figure out what to do with her once she is required to leave the temple. The image of the dove is also meaningful and offers a strong symbolic connection to Mary, as she is fed like a dove by a heavenly angel in 8:2. Evoking ideas of purity and innocence, the dove serves to highlight Mary's virginity and alludes to the unconventional nature of her relationship to Joseph.

B. *high priest:* here both de Strycker and Tischendorf have only "priest" but high priest is attested in various other manuscripts.

C. *Joseph, Joseph:* so de Strycker (from P. Bodmer V). Tischendorf lacks mention of Joseph's name and various manuscripts mention it only once or triple the reference.

D. *virgin of the Lord:* Mary is given this special title for the first time in the scene clarifying her post-temple fate. Note that now Mary's purity is almost exclusively discussed in terms of her sexual purity rather than, as earlier expressed, her ritual purity (Vuong, *Gender and Purity*, 161–92). Parallels have also been suggested between Mary's title and Roman traditions surrounding vestal virgins. Virginity functions as the basic criteria for both positions and both are iconic roles belonging both to the deity and the people. One critical distinguishing marker between the two positions is that vestal virgins have priestly obligations and are given privileges connected to this role. While Mary surely is raised in the temple, there is no indication that she serves as a priest or is required to fulfill any priestly obligations.

E. *guardianship:* the reference to guardianship makes clear from the onset that Joseph's primary role is to protect and guard Mary. While the narrative still labels the relationship between Mary and Joseph a betrothal, there is a clear sense that the traditional involvements of a marriage are not the intention.

(2) [8]But Joseph protested, saying, "I have sons and I am an old man;[A] she is only a girl.[B] I object lest I become a laughingstock to the children of Israel." [9]The high priest[C] answered, "Joseph, fear the Lord your God, and remember what God did to Dathan, Abiron, and Kore[D]—how the earth was split open and they were all swallowed up because of their protest. [10]Now be afraid, Joseph, lest these things also happen in your house."

(3) [11]And Joseph was afraid[E] and took her into his guardianship. [12]He said to her, "Mary,[F] I received you from the Lord's

cf. Num 16:1–35; 26:9

A. *old man:* Joseph's self-designation as old as justification for why he cannot take on Mary as a wife is reinforced more emphatically in other texts and translations. In the Armenian versions (4.2, 4; Terian, *Armenian Gospel*, 153), for instance, Joseph brings a cane rather than a rod. In *Hist. Jos. Carp.* 14, Joseph is 40 when he marries, 89 when his wife dies, and 90 when he is chosen by lot to care for Mary. Cf. Mark 6:3 and Matt 13:55–56 that mention Jesus' brothers and sisters but do not articulate their relationship or connection to Joseph. Additionally, Matt 1:18–19 and Luke 2:5 seem to depict Joseph as of marriageable age, a sharp contrast to the elderly figure described here.

B. *I have sons and I am an old man; she is only a girl:* the three details contained in Joseph's response (already having children, being elderly, and referring to Mary as a child) function to reinforce Mary's pure status as unjeopardized. In other words, Joseph is not a traditional spouse with conjugal rights to Mary, but functions solely as her protector. The depiction of Joseph as having children from a previous marriage and Joseph's embarrassment to be seen with someone of Mary's age supports this reading and is used to alleviate the concern that readers might have surrounding the naming of the arrangement between Mary and Joseph as a marriage.

C. *high priest:* de Strycker (following P. Bodmer V) and Tischendorf have only "priest."

D. *Dathan, Abiron, and Kore:* Dathan, Abiron, and Kore were swallowed whole by the earth for offering improper sacrifices by way of "strange fire." The comparison likens Joseph's rejection of the arrangement sanctioned by God to the offering of idols. Indeed the acts of Levi's sons necessitate a single priestly line, thus drawing the connection between Joseph and Aaron even closer: both Aaron and Joseph are chosen by lot by means of a rod to care for and protect the temple and Mary (the symbolic temple), respectively.

E. *Joseph was afraid:* Joseph's decision to agree to the arrangements is wholly based on fear, reinforcing that the betrothal between himself and Mary is not meant to be interpreted as a common marriage (see note on 9:8 above). Indeed, Joseph never refers outright to Mary as his wife (γυνή) throughout the entire narrative (cf. 17:2–4 and 19:5–8 in which Joseph struggles to come up with a proper way of explaining his relationship to Mary).

F. *He said to her, Mary:* εἶπεν αὐτῇ · Μαρία, so de Strycker (following P.

temple, but now I am leaving you[A] in my house[B] because I am going out to build some houses, but I will come back to you. The Lord will keep watch over you."[C]

10 (1) [1]Now[D] there was a council of the priests, saying, "We should make a curtain[E] for the temple of the Lord."[F] [2]Then the

---

Bodmer V). Tischendorf has εἶπεν Ἰωσὴφ τῇ Μαρίαμ · Ἰδού ("Joseph said to Mary, "Behold"").

A. *I received you from the Lord's temple . . . I am leaving you:* these are the only words Joseph speaks to Mary before he departs from her. Joseph's decision to depart almost immediately after taking Mary in, thus leaving her to fend for herself, may strike the reader as odd since he was just chosen by lot to take her into his care and protection. However, their limited interaction intentionally reinforces the idea that Mary belongs more to the Lord than to Joseph, eliminating any possibility of a sexual relationship; indeed, when addressing Mary, Joseph repeats her title as the Lord's virgin and leaves her in God's care.

B. *my house:* the assumption is that Mary has moved to Joseph's home located somewhere in Jerusalem.

C. *the Lord will keep watch over you:* the protection of the Lord is a common biblical motif. E.g., LXX Gen 28:15, 28:20, LXX Ps 30:3, 41:2, 90:11 and Luke 4:10.

D. *now:* some translators have suggested this scene occurs simultaneously with Joseph's leaving of Mary, but the precise amount of time that has elapsed is not indicated. Given the narrative flow, however, an almost immediate time frame is likely.

E. *curtain:* the commissioning of a new temple curtain is often cited as evidence for the author's lack of familiarity with temple practices. The text, however, does not explicitly state that the call is for the creation of the first temple curtain. The Mishnah and Talmud attest to the creation of replacement veils in which 82 virgins participate in its making. During times in which the temple was plundered and looted and the veil removed, a replacement veil would be commissioned at the rededication of the temple. Antiochus Epiphanes IV, for instance, is said to have specifically removed the temple curtain alongside other temple valuables including the golden altar, the lampstand for the light, and all its utensils (i.e., 1 Macc 1:20–23). However, a replacement veil was rehung once the temple was taken back by the Maccabees (1 Macc 4:51). Josephus provides a similar account of the pillaging of the temple with specific reference to the removal of the veil, noting both Antiochus Epiphanes (*A.J.* 12.5.4 [250]) as well as the destruction of the Second Temple in 70 CE (*B.J.* 6.8.3 [389]).

F. *we should make a curtain for the temple of the Lord:* the decision to create a temple curtain becomes the impetus for inviting Mary back to the temple despite the threat she poses to its purity; her good standing is thus affirmed. On the Holy of Holies' curtain, cf. Exod 26:31, 36; 35:25; 36:35; 2 Chr

high priest[A] said, "Call to me the undefiled virgins[B] from the tribe of David."[C] [3]And the (temple) officers departed and searched and found seven virgins.[D] [4]And the high priest[E] remembered the child Mary,[F] that she was also from the tribe of David[G] and was un-

---

3:14. Curtains were not uncommon as protectors and barriers for holy items and spaces. Exod 26:1, for instance, describes the tabernacle being built with ten curtains made of fine twisted blue, purple, and crimson yarn, and Exod 30:6 describes a curtain that must be used to shelter the ark.

A. *high priest*: de Strycker (following P. Bodmer V) and Tischendorf have only "priest."

B. *undefiled virgins*: a couple of Tischendorf's manuscripts specify seven virgins (ἑπτὰ παρθένους).

C. *undefiled virgins from the tribe of David*: the undefiled virgins recalls Mary's playmates at 6:5 who are sexually and likely ritually pure; but the added criteria of Davidic lineage heightens Mary's special status by drawing a direct connection between her and the royal line of David. Cf. Matt 1:1–16 and Luke 3:23–38, which connect Jesus' Davidic lineage through his adoptive father.

D. *seven virgins*: ἑπτὰ παρθένους, so Tischendorf. De Strycker (following P. Bodmer V) has simply "seven." An especially sacred number in Scripture, seven is intentionally used here to emphasize the holiness of the curtain used for the temple. See 6:2 when Mary walks seven steps before she is lifted up by her mother. Note, though, that with the addition of Mary, there are eight weavers in total. Mary's elevated status allows her to join what is already a complete set of seven spinners; remembered as the most important of the virgins and descendants of David, Mary cannot be left out and in fact is chosen by lot to spin the most significant threads.

E. *high priest*: de Strycker (following P. Bodmer V) and Tischendorf have only "priest."

F. *the child Mary*: the (high) priest's reference to Mary as a child (παιδός), despite their arrangement to have her betrothed to Joseph, strengthens the view that Mary does not function as a traditional wife.

G. *she was also from the tribe of David*: Mary is remembered and invited back to the temple by the same priests who requested her departure, reinforcing Mary's purity as intact and confirming her royal lineage. While the reference to the "tribe of David" is problematic inasmuch as there did not exist a tribe so-named among the Israelites, the narrative intention seems simply to indicate Davidic lineage or the tribe to which David belonged—i.e., Judah. The reference to the tribe of David here and earlier at 10:2 is clearly meant to depict Mary as responsible for carrying on the Davidic lineage rather than Joseph. In this way, Jesus' connection to David is direct rather than adoptive, drawing the messianic connection closer. Cf. Luke 1:5 and 1:36 where Mary's lineage is traced through the line of Aaron instead. That Jesus' relationship to David is only adoptive, according to Matthew and Luke, seems to have concerned some early Christian writers like Ignatius of Antioch and Justin

defiled in God's sight.ᴬ ⁵And the (temple) officers departed and brought her back.

(2) ⁶And they led them into the Lord's temple.⁷And the high priestᴮ said, "Cast lots before meᶜ to determine who will spin the gold, white,ᴰ and the linen, and the silk, and the violet-blue, the scarlet, and the pure purple."ᴱ ⁸And Mary drew the lot for the

cf. Exod 26:31–36; 35:25; 37:6

Martyr, who also made claims of Mary's direct connection to the royal line— e.g., Ignatius, *Eph.* 18.2 and Justin, *Dial.* 43, 45, 100, 120, respectively. See also the explicit reference to Mary as descendant from the "seed of David, when the Holy Spirit was sent from Heaven by the Father into her. . ." in *3 Corinthians* and later Maximus the Confessor's *Life of the Virgin*, where Mary is linked to the Davidic line: "[Mary] too was from the house and family of David" (33; ed. Shoemaker).

A. *undefiled in God's sight:* ἀμίαντος with the use of the dative can indicate Mary's purity on multiple levels; namely not only is she virginally pure, but also ritually pure. Cf. 6:5, 7:4, and 10:2 where ἀμίαντος draws upon both meanings of purity. While the seven other virgins chosen meet the criteria of being sexually pure and of the line of David, it is unlikely they maintained the heightened level of ritual purity exemplified by Mary's upbringing, which only strengthens her superior status within the elite group of virgins and justifies why she among all virgins is chosen to be the Lord's Virgin.

B. *high priest:* de Strycker (following P. Bodmer V) and Tischendorf have only "priest."

C. *cast lots:* the casting of lots is a popular motif in biblical literature to express God's complete control, rather than suggesting random selection as today. Lots were cast to resolve various issues, such as division of land (Josh 14–21), division of priestly and temple duties (1 Chr 24:5, 31; 25:8–9; 26:13–14), the appointment or replacement of positions (Acts 1:26), etc. In this case, the casting of lots to determine what threads Mary will weave is significant and again speaks to her special status, recalling 8:8 when Joseph is chosen by lot to guard Mary and foreshadowing 24:13 when the lot falls upon Simeon to replace Zachariah's position.

D. *white:* ἀμίαντος is used five times throughout the *Protevangelium.* The term is often used to describe a person, i.e., "undefiled daughters of the Hebrews" (6:5; 7:4); "undefiled virgins from the tribe of David" (10:2); or Mary as "undefiled in God's sight" (10:4). Here it is used to describe the threads used for the temple veil. ἀμίαντος is also a fine variety of asbestos. Asbestos fibers come in five colors: white, red, blue, brown, and green. Given the text's concern for purity, white is the preferred translation for the color of the threads.

E. *gold . . . pure purple:* seven colors are listed with regard to the threads used on the veil; however, eight virgins (seven plus Mary) are tasked with the veil's creation. The text does not offer a solution as to how the colors are distributed after Mary is given both the pure purple and scarlet threads, leaving five colors to be shared among the remaining seven virgins. Cf. Exod. 26:31

pure purple and scarlet threads[A] and she took them and went to her house. [9]Now it was at this time that Zechariah became mute and Samuel took his place,[B] until Zechariah could speak again. [10](Meanwhile) Mary took the scarlet and was spinning[C] it.

cf. Luke 1:20–22, 64

---

and 2 Chr 3:14, in which four colors (blue, scarlet, purple, and linen) are used to create the first temple veil. Philo (*Mos.* 2.88) and Josephus (*B.J.* 5.5.4 [213]) both comment on the symbolism behind the use of these four colors: linen (earth), purple (water), blue (air), and scarlet (fire).

A. *pure purple and scarlet threads*: the color purple symbolizes royalty and riches, appropriately assigned to Mary to highlight her royal lineage and recall her wealthy parents' background (1:1). Despite being among other virgins who similarly share a royal Davidic lineage, Mary's lineage is featured prominently as the most royal (cf. Exod 26:1; 27:16; 2 Chr 2:14; Judg 8:26; Prov 31:22; Luke 16:19; and Mark 15:17, 20 for the use of purple for the tabernacle, temple, royal gowns, the garments of the wealthy, and Jesus' robe). In the HB and NT, the color scarlet is connected to ideas of cleansing and purification (Lev 14:4, 52; Num 19:6; Heb 9:19), but also with the virtuous (Prov 31:21). This color thread is another fitting choice for Mary given that she is likened to a temple sacrifice by way of her parent's careful raising of their daughter, but also that she consistently emerges as the most pure and pious character in the narrative. Biblical usage of scarlet is also attested in Gen 38:28–30 and Josh 2:18 in the context of scarlet cords, but also 2 Sam 1:24 and Prov 31:21 as a sign of prosperity. Jesus' robe is also described as scarlet in Matt 27:28.

B. *Zechariah became mute and Samuel took his place*: this awkward injection of a somewhat unrelated scene about Zechariah becoming mute may be an attempt by the author to connect his narrative to the story of Jesus' birth, which in Luke begins with the account of the miraculous birth of Zechariah's and Elizabeth's son, John (Luke 1:20–22, 64).

C. *spinning*: Mary's working of the threads for the temple curtain is narratively woven into the Annunciation scene itself. Appearing in three significant positions—before the bodiless voice, before the appearance of the physical angel, and immediately after the departure of the angel—the subtle references to her spinning function to reinforce as well as justify Mary's special, blessed status. Whether the depiction of Mary spinning is apologetic (responding to hostile claims about her status; see *Cels.* 1.28–32) or for the purpose of encomium (see Hock, *Infancy Gospels*, 15–21), the image becomes an iconic way of artistically depicting the Virgin (see Mary in Art in Introduction).

11 (1) ¹And she took the water pitcher and went out^A and filled it with water.^B ²And behold, there was a voice saying,^C "Greetings, favored one! The Lord is with you. You are blessed among wom-en." ³And Mary looked all around her,^D to the right and left, to see

Luke 1:28

Luke 1:42

A. *she took the water pitcher and went out:* the depiction of Mary outside in public space contrasts sharply with the secure and protected world of her childhood bedroom-turned-sanctuary and the sacred Jerusalem temple. The idea that virgins should be kept indoors for fear that the outside world is too risky since virgins are especially tempting to sexually dangerous men is a common motif found not only among biblical stories (e.g., Sus 15–17) and early church fathers (e.g., Tertullian's *Virg.* 2), but also Greco-Roman novellas (e.g., *Leucippe and Clitophon* and *Daphnis and Chloe*). As a designated *parthenos*, the threat of physical danger and the jeopardizing of virginity are serious concerns, but since Mary is given the special status of Virgin of the Lord, she is safeguarded from the dangers that normally fall upon virgins who risk being outdoors—namely, rape and seduction. The special status itself functions in much the same way as the sacred walls of the temple to protect her from the gaze of uncontrollable male sexual desire.

B. *filled it with water:* the specifics of Mary's water source are not detailed by the narrator, but the positioning of Mary's pregnancy at a source of water (well-spring?) reinforces the parallel between Mary's productive potential and a well-spring. Likening Mary's womb to a water source is a popular motif particularly among Syrian churches and especially in connection with the celebration of the Feast of the Nativity. Ephrem the Syrian often drew analogies between living water and Mary's womb as a way to exalt her status: "she is a pure spring which has been mingled with the flow of marital union . . ." (*Hymns on Mary*, no. 15; Brock, *Bride of Light*, 80). In a homily, Jacob of Serugh carries on the spring-womb tradition by comparing Mary to a "new well" from which living water gushes forth. The motif of going to a water source and finding more than water is, of course, well known in biblical narrative: Jacob, Isaac, and Moses all to go wells and return with wives, thus achieving spiritual marriages.

C. *a voice saying:* the bodiless voice initiates the two-staged annunciation scene wherein Mary is told of her blessed status. The second stage commences when she returns to her house and physically encounters an angel of the Lord. The heavenly voice that greets and blesses Mary at the well reinforces her special status but also the safe space she occupies at this moment, despite having been removed from the guardianship of her parents, the priests, or even Joseph. This scene may be depicted in the third-century house church in Dura-Europos, possibly one of the earliest extant house churches from antiquity. See Mary in Art in the Introduction.

D. *Mary looked all around her:* whether this bodiless voice comes from the angel or God is unclear. Given that the angel physically appears to her almost immediately after she returns home encourages the reading that it is the angel's voice, but the voice of God (*bat kol*) should not be dismissed since there are various rabbinic traditions associated with the voice of God

from where the voice was coming. ⁴And she began trembling and went into her house^A and put the water pitcher down. And taking up the purple (thread) she sat down on her chair and began to spin the purple (thread).^B

(2) ⁵And behold, an angel stood before her^C saying, "Do not be afraid, Mary,^D for you have found favor before the Master of all. You will conceive from his Word." ⁶But when she heard this, Mary doubted herself^E and said, "If I conceive by the Lord, the living God, will I give birth^F like all other women give birth?"^G

Luke 1:30–31; cf. Judg 13:3–5

cf. Luke 1:34

(Zervos, "Annunciation," 682–86). Cf. Jesus' baptism scene: Mark 1:9–11 par.

A. *she began trembling and went into her house:* Mary's frightened reaction and immediate return home reinforces her human qualities, as most people would respond in fear to strange bodiless voices and seek the shelter of their private home. On the other hand, her frequent interactions with the angelic being during her stay in the temple should have prepared her in some way for the appearance of the angel before her.

B. *purple (thread):* the repeated reference to Mary's working of the purple threads serves as a subtle reminder of Mary's royal blood, connection to the Davidic line, and her special status even among other virgins. These particular characteristics, suggested just prior to the appearance of the heavenly messenger, highlight why she among all others is chosen and remind readers of her close connection to the temple even if she no longer lives there. What is more, the threads spun by Mary for the creation of the temple veil at the moment of the annunciation additionally connect Mary's unborn child to the temple and reinforce the idea that the temple veil and Jesus' earthly body are created at the same time by Mary, but also that they will be torn at the same time at Jesus' crucifixion (cf. Mark 15:38 par.).

C. *an angel stood before her:* the second stage of the Annunciation takes place when a physical being appears before Mary to speak to her. Achieving what the bodiless voice was unable to do in the first attempt to interact with Mary, the angelic figure successfully carries out his duty to deliver the heavenly message. *angel:* so de Strycker (from P. Bodmer V). Some of Tischendorf's manuscripts add "of the Lord."

D. *Do not be afraid, Mary:* the *Protevangelium* does not include Luke's reference to the naming and meaning of Jesus, his ancestral connection to David, and his reign over the house of Jacob is absent. Instead, the message delivered to Mary simply details precisely what Mary's role as the Virgin of the Lord entails: having being set aside as God's favored one, Mary's primary role is to conceive and bear the child of God.

E. *Mary doubted herself:* note that the doubt centers not in the conception, but about the manner in which she will give birth.

F. *will I give birth:* καὶ γεννήσω, so Tischendorf. Lacking in de Strycker (and P. Bodmer V).

G. *like all other women give birth:* As one of the few times she speaks in

(3) ⁷And the angel of the Lord said to her,ᴬ "Not in this way,
Luke 1:35 Mary, because the power of God will overshadow you.ᴮ Therefore
the holy one born from you will be called the Son of the Most
Luke 1:32 High.ᶜ And you will name him Jesus for he will save his people
Matt 1:21 from their sins."ᴰ ⁸And Mary replied, "Behold, the slave of the
Luke 1:31, 38 Lord is before him. Let it happen to me according to your word."ᴱ

12 (1) ¹And she made the purple and scarletᶠ and brought them
to the temple. ²And the high priestᴳ took it, blessed it,ᴴ and said,

---

the narrative, Mary is revealed as a thoughtful individual who ponders the
logistics of the angel's proposal. Accepting the idea that she will not conceive
like other women, Mary naturally asks whether the next step in pregnancy
will also be accomplished through regular means. Once Mary is told that all
aspects of her experience will be unique to her alone, she accepts the angel's
message willingly.

A. *And the angel of the Lord said to her:* so Tischendorf. De Strycker
(following P. Bodmer V) has καὶ ἰδοὺ ἄγγελος ἔστη αὐτῇ λέγων αὐτῇ. ("And
behold, and an angel appeared to her saying to her"). Given that the angel
has already appeared before Mary and is in the middle of responding to her
question, the variant reading here is preferred.

B. *the power of God will overshadow you:* δύναμις γὰρ Θεοῦ ἐπισκιάσει.
Some manuscripts have ἀλλὰ πνεῦμα ἅγίον ἐπελεύσεται ἐπί σε καὶ δύναμις
ὑψίστου ἐπισκιάσει σοι ("but the Holy Spirit will come upon you and the
power of the Most High will overshadow you"), an effort to harmonize the
text with Luke 1:35.

C. *Most High:* ὑψίστου. Some manuscripts have Θεοῦ, thus, "Son of God."

D. *you will name him Jesus . . . sins:* the naming and the explanation of
Jesus' name is taken verbatim from Matthew, albeit to Joseph rather than,
as here, to Mary. In Luke, the naming of Jesus is connected to the Son of the
Most High (1:32) and Son of God (1:35) rather than to his role as a savior of
all "people from their sins."

E. *according to your word:* while there is no description of how the conception takes place, the idea that Mary's conception took place through the ear
is a common belief in late antique and medieval sources. See Murray, "Mary,
the Second Eve," 372–84; and Rosenberg, "Penetrating Words," 127–31.

F. *purple and scarlet:* this third mention of Mary's spinning (cf. 10:10 and
11:4) completes the sandwiched references to Mary's connection to the Davidic line and her virtuous status as virgin, but also returns the priesthood to
the scene by confirming their approval of Mary and her new role, given that
they immediately bless and praise her.

G. *high priest:* de Strycker (following P. Bodmer V) and Tischendorf have
only "priest."

H. *took it, blessed it:* λαβὼν ὁ ἱερεὺς εὐλόγησεν αὐτὴν, so de Strycker (from
P. Bodmer V). Tischendorf lacks "taking." The object here (αὐτὴν) could also

"Mary, the Lord God has magnified your name and you will be blessed among all the generations of the earth."[A] cf. Luke 1:46

(2) ³Mary rejoiced and went to her kinswoman Elizabeth.[B] ⁴She knocked on the door; when Elizabeth heard her she tossed aside the scarlet[C] and ran to the door and opened it for her. ⁵And she blessed her[D] and said, "How is it that the mother of my Lord should come to me? For behold, the child in me sprang up and

---

be translated "her"; thus, the priest would be blessing Mary.

A. *blessed among all the generations of the earth*: the priest's immediate praising and blessing of Mary's contribution to the temple curtain reinforce the positioning of the priests as continued supporters of Mary, despite their participation in her removal at 8:4. Similarly to her son whose name is also praised, Mary's name is specifically expanded by the priests to include sanctification by all the generations of the earth, enlarging the scope of the heavenly angel's words at the Annunciation. Cf. Luke 1:46, 48 which recalls the idea of magnification and favor, although Mary is the one praising rather than being praised.

B. *Elizabeth*: Elizabeth is abruptly introduced in this scene. In Luke 1:5, Elizabeth is a descendant of Aaron. Given Zechariah's priestly appointment both in the *Protevangelium* and in Luke, both of John's parents are thus portrayed as descending from priestly families. While Elizabeth's lineage is not noted in the narrative, her relation to Mary is, making Elizabeth also of Davidic lineage since Mary is emphatically noted as a descendant.

C. *she tossed aside the scarlet*: Elizabeth too may have been chosen to help weave the temple curtain. This detail, attested in numerous manuscripts, poses a problem in that part of the requirements for those chosen to weave involves being a pure virgin from the tribe of David. While her married and pregnant status disqualifies Elizabeth from the ranks of virgins, the intention here may simply be to reinforce the closeness between Mary and the Davidic line and the uprightness of her companions even in adulthood since loom work was often associated with the virtuous; also perhaps the closeness between Jesus and John by way of their mothers is alluded to here.

D. *she blessed her*: εὐλόγησεν αὐτήν, so de Strycker (from P. Bodmer V). Tischendorf has ἰδοῦσα τὴν Μαριὰμ εὐλόγησεν αὐτήν ("seeing Mary, she blessed her").

Luke 1:39–43
cf. Luke 1:19, 26

Luke 1:56 blessed you."ᴬ ⁶But Mary forgot the mysteriesᴮ that the angelᶜ Gabriel had spoken, and she looked up to heaven and said, "Who am I, Lord,ᴰ that all the womenᴱ of the earth should bless me?"

(3) ⁷And she stayed three months with Elizabeth. ⁸Day by day her belly grew. And Mary became frightened, returned home, and hid herself from the children of Israel. ⁹And she was sixteen years oldᶠ when all these mysteries happened to her.

A. *the child in me sprang up and blessed you:* after receiving blessings from the high priest for her work in which her specific name is to be extolled, Mary receives two more blessings: the first by her kinswoman Elizabeth; and second, by Elizabeth's unborn child (the future John the Baptist). These blessings emphatically confirm Mary's special status, perhaps a necessary reminder given that accusations challenging her character occur hereafter. *sprang up:* ἐσκίρτησεν. Some manuscripts have ἐν τῇ κοιλίᾳ μου ("in my belly") and ἐν ἀγαλλιάσει ("in exaltation") or a combination of both.

B. *Mary forgot the mysteries:* Mary's odd memory lapse of the conversation she engaged in with the angel occasions much speculation. Some suggestions for understanding this unusual detail include its function as a narrative device to further confirm Mary's pure status; others have suggested that it allows for a sort of harmonizing of the elements of the narrative that parallel details in Matthew (and Luke); namely, it allows Joseph to receive his dream-revelation.

C. *angel:* so de Strycker (from P. Bodmer V). Tischendorf's manuscripts identify Gabriel more specifically as an ἀρχάγγελος ("archangel").

D. *Who am I, Lord:* de Strycker (following P. Bodmer V) lacks "Lord" (Κύριε), reading instead τίς εἰμι ἐγὼ ὅτι ἰδού. ("who am I, that behold").

E. *all the women:* most manuscripts replace αἱ γυναῖκες ("women," as in P. Bodmer V) with αἱ γενεαί ("generations") perhaps to reflect the original blessing by the high priest at 12:2. The chosen reading makes the blessing of Mary's motherhood by all women (thus mothers/potential mothers) more poignant.

F. *was sixteen years old:* while δέκα ἕξ (sixteen) is attested in the majority of the manuscripts, twelve, fourteen, fifteen, and seventeen are also attested. Considering the reference to Mary's age of twelve at 8:3, if Mary were sixteen years old when she encountered Gabriel, Joseph would have been physically absent from his home and Mary for approximately four years. The general acceptance of sixteen years old is accounted for in various ways. Based on the description by Luke as well as Mary's visit with Elizabeth, the time lapse between 9:3 and 13:1 could not be less than six months or more than four years (Smid, *Protevangelium Jacobi*, 92). It has also been suggested that the reference to the age of sixteen might be caused by the author forgetting he has already indicated Mary's age of twelve at 8:3 (de Strycker, *La forme la plus ancienne*, 411). This later explanation is harder to digest given the stress on Mary's age by the priests (they repeat Mary's age of twelve twice in the same verse) as the reason she must leave the temple. Some have argued that the

13 (1) ¹When she was in her sixth month, behold, Joseph came home from his building, and entered his house, and found Mary pregnant. ²He struck himself in the face and threw himself to the ground in sackcloth, and wailed bitterly saying, "How can I face the Lord God? ³What kind of prayer can I make about her^A since I received her^B as a virgin from the temple of the Lord God and I did not protect her.^C ⁴Who has conspired against me?^D Who has done this evil deed in my house? Who took the virgin away from me and defiled her?^E ⁵Could it be that the story of Adam^F is being repeated in my case? For just as Adam was in the hour of his praising when the serpent came and found Eve alone and deceived her and defiled her,^G so too has the same happened to me." cf. Gen 3:1–20

younger ages of twelve and fourteen are more reasonable if the accusations against Joseph are to be viewed as serious (Hock, *Infancy Gospels*, 55).

A. *about her*: περὶ αὐτῆς, so de Strycker (from P. Bodmer V). Tischendorf has περὶ τῆς κόρης ταύτης ("about this girl"). Some manuscripts have the synonym νεάνιδος.

B. *her*: αὐτήν, a variant found in P. Bodmer V and Tischendorf's manuscripts, which has been used here for clarity's sake. De Strycker omits.

C. *I did not protect her*: Joseph's initial response upon finding that Mary is pregnant is interesting in that it may speak to the irregularity of their relationship, especially since he had already handed over the responsibility of caring for Mary to the Lord (9:12). Unlike a traditional marriage, Joseph's response is not to the possibility that Mary is an adulteress, but that he would be blamed by the priests and Israel as a whole for failing to protect her, as he was chosen by lot to do.

D. *Who has conspired against me*: τίς ὁ θηρεύσας με. Literally, "Who has hunted me?"

E. *Who took the virgin away from me and defiled her*: so de Strycker. Tischendorf and P. Bodmer V preserve only the last portion of this sentence ("and defiled her"), though for αὐτήν ("her") Tischendorf has τὴν παρθένον ("the virgin").

F. *story of Adam*: Joseph's self-comparison to Adam by association conjures comparisons between Mary and Eve and the popular motif of Mary as the Second Eve. Eve as the mother of all living humans and Mary as the mother of Christ, these women stand as the most important female figures in Christian history. See, e.g., Justin Martyr, *Dial.* 100; Irenaeus, *Haer.* 22, and Tertullian, *Carn. Chr.* 17, where this typology is further explored in that Eve's disobedience and contribution to human death is sharply contrasted with Mary's complete obedience and role in salvation history.

G. *and defiled her*: καὶ ἐμίανεν αὐτήν, so de Strycker (from P. Bodmer V). Lacking in Tischendorf. The addition of "defile" to the act of deception acted upon Eve by the serpent makes explicit the idea that Joseph's accusation

(2) [6]Then Joseph stood up from the sackcloth and called Mary and said to her, "You who have been cared for by God—

cf. Gen 4:13 why have you done this?[A] [7]Have you forgotten the Lord your God? Why have you shamed your soul—you who were raised in the Holy of Holies[B] and received food from the hand of an angel?"[C]

(3) [8]But she wailed bitterly and said, "I am pure and have not

cf. Luke 1:34 known a man (sexually)."[d] [9]And Joseph said to her,[e] "How then

---

against Mary involves a sexual affair. The point, of course, is that the possible sexual seduction of Eve by the serpent (a common trope in Syriac Christianity; see Minov, "'Serpentine' Eve," 102 and Rosenberg, "Sexual Serpents," 480) functions as a foil to Mary's paradoxical body, both virgin and mother.

A. *why have you done this:* the question Joseph poses to Mary is the very same one God asks Eve in Gen 2:13, but also the same as that posed to Mary and Joseph by the high priest later. The questioning of Mary's sexual status after Joseph has taken her in is at odds with traditions surrounding marriage whereby the questioning of one's virginal status occurs before the marriage takes place.

B. *raised in the Holy of Holies:* in his accusation against Mary, Joseph repeats precisely the reasons why Mary cannot be found guilty: Mary is the purest of pure, raised in the Holy of Holies, and fed by a heavenly messenger. Joseph's accusation also draws out a concern for Mary's innocence in addition to her purity, thus the text for the first time opens up for discussion, if only for a short time, the possibility of Mary's interaction with moral and sexual impurity—an impurity of the flesh caused by the sexual act. These are much more serious than the impurity caused by natural and unpreventable impurities since they cannot be absolved simply though the participation in certain rituals dictated by Levitical law.

C. *received food from the hand of an angel:* lacking in P. Ashmolean. Its absence also in the Syriac and two Armenian versions has convinced Bingen ("Protévangile de Jacques," 206) that this reading is a variant rather than a scribal error.

D. *I am pure. And I have not known a man sexually:* Mary's minimal verbal role in the narrative (she speaks only eight times throughout the entire narrative) here reinforces the importance of her self-declaration and defense of her purity and innocence.

E. *And Joseph said to her:* P. Ashmolean adds ἀποκριθ[ε]ὶς (answered) before εἶπεν αὐτῇ Ἰωσήφ.

are you pregnant?" [10]And she answered, "As the Lord my God lives,[a] I do not know from where it came to me."[b]

14 (1) [1]Then Joseph was very frightened and kept quiet from her,[c] considering carefully[D] what to do about her. [2]And Joseph said to himself,[E] "If I keep her sin[F] a secret, I will be found in opposition[G] to the law of the Lord; [3]but if I expose her condition to the children of Israel, I fear that perhaps the child inside her is angelic[H] and I will be found handing over innocent blood[I] to a

A. *As the Lord my God lives:* according to Mesopotamian law, the only discernable way to prove one's virginity is by way of swearing an oath (Cooper, "Virginity in Mesopotamia," 91–112). As a phrase commonly used to initiate oaths (see note on 4:2 above and Anna's vow), Mary is willing to swear by God to verify her virginity, even if it falls upon deaf ears.

B. *I do not know from where it came to me:* narratively, Mary's memory lapse also functions to make her declaration of innocence and purity more emphatic since the discourse of accusation would be unnecessary if Mary simply remembered her conversation with Gabriel.

C. *kept quiet from her:* ἠρεμεῖν is also used at 18:4 to render quiet; however, the term is rarely attested in the *Protevangelium* and its meaning is obscure in this context. For this reason, some have preferred the translation "kept away from her" in terms of a physical separation as if he were abstaining from conjugal relations with her. This, however, is a more problematic translation since there seems to be no indication Mary and Joseph ever engaged in any marital relations. The intended sense seems to be that Joseph wants to refrain from making a decision, opting rather to stay "quiet" instead (see de Strycker, *La forme la plus ancienne,* 304–5).

D. *considering carefully:* P. Ashmolean attests to καὶ ἐβουλεύσατο ("and planned") instead of διαλογιζόμενος.

E. *to himself:* ἐν ἑαυτῷ, is attested in various manuscripts, though not P. Bodmer V and not in the editions of de Strycker nor Tischendorf. The variant reading is preferred since it is clear that Joseph is speaking to himself.

F. *her sin:* P. Ashmolean attributes the sin to Joseph instead of Mary: ἁμάρτημα ποιῶ ("the sin I committed"). Bingen ("Protévangile de Jacques," 208, 212) argues that the text has been reworked in order to keep the blame consistent since Joseph is accused by the priest at 15:16 not to bear false witness.

G. *opposition:* μαχόμενος. Some manuscripts have ἔνοχος ("held in or bound") by the law of the Lord.

H. *angelic:* ἀγγελικόν. Some manuscripts have ἅγιον ("holy").

I. *handing over innocent blood:* Joseph's fear of betraying Mary evokes Judas's repenting of his betrayal of Jesus.

death sentence. ⁴What then should I do with her? I will secretly divorce her."ᴬ

cf. Matt 27:
cf. Matt 1:1

(2) ⁵And night laid hold of him, and behold, an angel of the Lord appeared to himᴮ in a dream and said,ᶜ "Do not be afraid of this child,ᴰ for that which is inside her is from the Holy Spirit. ⁶She will have a sonᴱ and you will name him Jesus; for he will save his people from their sins."ꜰ ⁷And Joseph arose from his sleep and glorified the God of Israel for showing him favor. ⁸And he guarded the child.ᴳ

cf. Matt 1:20–21
cf. Matt 1:24

cf. Luke 3:2;
John 18:13

15 (1) ¹But Annas the scribeᴴ came to him and said to him, "Joseph, why have you not attended our council?" ²And he replied to

A. *I will secretly divorce her*: given the untraditional conditions of their relationship and that no reference is made to a formal marriage, Joseph's comment on divorcing Mary appears problematic since it implies that they were married. The intention of the statement may simply be that Joseph wants to cut ties with Mary rather than referencing a more formal divorce. This reading is supported by the consistent depiction of Mary's purity but also by 19:5–11, wherein Joseph offers a bumbling and confusing description of his relationship to Mary to the Hebrew midwife.

B. *an angel of the Lord appeared to him*: it is not Mary's swearing of her virginity that convinces Joseph of her innocence, but the divine intervention of God via the sending of his angel to explain the situation.

C. *in a dream and said*: κατ' ὄνειρον vs. the more ubiquitous κατ' ὄναρ.

D. *Do not be afraid of this child*: the angel repeatedly refers to Mary as a child as if to reinforce the uncomfortable difference between her age and Joseph's.

E. *She will have a son*: τέξεται δὲ σοι υἱόν, so de Strycker (from P. Bodmer V). P. Ashmolean omits σοι.

F. *for he will save his people from their sins*: this precise information is addressed to Mary at 11:8.

G. *And he guarded the child*: given Joseph's almost immediate departure after receiving Mary into his home at 9:12, coupled with his initial objection to the result of the casting of lots at 9:8, the text suggests that Joseph did not wholly accept his position as Mary's guardian. However, after confronting Mary's pregnant state and receiving confirmation that Mary's child is in accordance with God's will via an angelic message in a dream, Joseph's statement that he will guard Mary seems now to be whole-hearted and sincere. *the child*: τὴν παῖδα, so de Strycker (from P. Bodmer V). Tischendorf has ("her").

H. *Annas the scribe*: *Inf. Gos. Thom.* 3:1 names Annas the scribe as the father whose son is cursed by Jesus. The name Annas and its connection to Jewish leadership in general may have been influenced by Luke 3:2 and John 18:13, who both connect the name Annas with the priesthood. Indeed, while Annas is described as a scribe he clearly has a close relationship to the

him, "I was weary from traveling on the road and I rested on the first day."ᴬ ³Then Annas turned and saw that Mary was pregnant.

(2) ⁴And he left and ran quickly to the high priestᴮ and said to him, "Behold,ᶜ Joseph—the one you vouched for—has committed a great transgression." ⁵And the high priestᴰ replied, "What has he done?" ⁶And he replied, "Joseph has defiled the virgin which he received from the temple of the Lord and he has stolen her wedding rightsᴱ but has not disclosed it to the children of Israel."ᶠ ⁷And the high priest said to him,ᴳ "Has Joseph done

---

priesthood since it is straight to the high priest to whom he reports his encounter with Joseph and Mary. P. Ashmolean, along with some Syriac manuscripts, includes a critical variant not found elsewhere in the Greek tradition, but suggested by Bingen to belong to an earlier (perhaps original) form of the text. It contains the end of a scene which expands upon Annas the scribe's questioning of Mary's and Joseph's situation: ναί ἵνα εἰδῇ[ς ὅτι τὸ ἀληθὲς λέγω] πέμψον τοὺς ὑπηρέτας καὶ [ε]ὑρή[σεις τὴν παρθένον ὡγ]κωμένην ("Yes. I [say this] so that you may know that I speak the truth; send your servants. You will find the virgin pregnant"). The presence of the word ναί seems to indicate that Annas the scribe had posed at least one question. For the reconstruction of this variant, see Bingen, "Protévangile de Jacques," 209.

A. *I rested on the first day:* the term ἀναπαύειν, here used to clearly indicate Joseph's need to rest because of his weary state, may help support the idea that the intention of the term also used in reference to Joachim at 4:10 is non-sexual.

B. *high priest:* de Strycker (following P. Bodmer V) and Tischendorf have only "priest." The identity of the high priest is unknown. The assumption is that it is Samuel who has taken Zechariah's place while he is mute (cf. 10:9).

C. *Behold:* ἰδού, so de Strycker (from P. Bodmer V). Lacking in Tischendorf.

D. *high priest:* here and throughout chaps. 15–16, so de Strycker (from P. Bodmer V). Tischendorf has "priest."

E. *stolen her wedding rights:* eloped or consummated the marriage.

F. *disclosed it to the children of Israel:* the irregularity of their relationship is again raised when the accusation against Mary and Joseph centers on the secret consummation of their marriage, as if Joseph actually had this right only if he revealed it to the children of Israel. While the original instructions by the angel at 8:8 indeed use the term wife (γυνή) to describe the arrangement, all references and descriptions of their relationship have urged the interpretation that Joseph serves as Mary's protector alone, including the instruction of the priests who make clear Joseph's role is limited to that of a guardian.

G. *the high priest said to him:* so de Strycker (from P. Bodmer V). Tischendorf has ἀποκριθεὶς ὁ ἱερεὺς εἶπεν ("answering, the priest said").

this?" [8]And he replied,[A] "Send servants and you will find the virgin pregnant."[B] [9]And the servants went forth and found her just as he had said. And they took her to the temple and she appeared in court, along with Joseph.[C]

(3) [10]And the high priest asked her, "Mary, why have you done this? Why have you humiliated your soul [11]and forgotten the Lord your God? You, who were raised in the Holy of Holies and received food from the hand of angels.[D] [12]You who heard their hymns and danced before them,[E] why have you done this?" [13]But she wept bitterly and said, "As the Lord God lives,[F] I am

cf. Luke 1:34 pure before him and have not known any man."[G]

A. *he replied*: so de Strycker (from P. Bodmer V). Tischendorf has "Annas the scribe replied."

B. *virgin pregnant*: Annas's accusations against both Mary and Joseph are based on the idea that a transgression has been made against Mary's role as the Virgin of the Lord. Annas's continual reference to Mary as a virgin despite his accusations seem to highlight Mary's paradoxical role as a pregnant virgin.

C. *temple . . . Joseph*: most witnesses simply have ἅμα τῷ Ἰωσὴφ εἰς τὸ κριτήριον ("along with Joseph into the court"). De Strycker (following P. Bodmer V) adds the reference to the temple: εἰς τὸ ἱερόν, καὶ ἔστη εἰς τὸ κριτήριον.

D. *angels*: so de Strycker (from P. Bodmer V). Tishendorf's manuscripts attest to a single angel.

E. *their hymns . . . before them*: so de Strycker (from P. Bodmer V). Tischendorf has Mary hearing *his* hymns and dancing before *him*.

F. *As the Lord God lives*: Mary's attempt to verify her virginity and innocence by way of an oath once again falls on deaf ears as the priests, much like Joseph, are unconvinced of her innocence. Thus she is required to undergo a physical ordeal dependent upon divine will and intervention to prove her sexual status as a virgin. The *Protevangelium* seems to value physical evidence over oaths as a method for determining virginity.

G. *I am pure before him and have not known any man*: Mary's response recalls the questioning of Gabriel on her condition despite not knowing a man at Luke 1:34. While Mary may have forgotten her conversation with the heavenly messenger (13:10), she speaks without hesitation for the fourth time here of her complete innocence and purity. Mary's testing by the high priest recalls the first test against her character when Joseph questions her pregnant condition (13:8). Her response to both tests is the declaration of her purity and innocence.

(4) [14]And the high priest said,[A] "Joseph, why have you done this?" [15]Joseph responded, "As the Lord my God lives,[B] and as his Christ lives, and the witness of his truth,[C] I am pure concerning her." [16]And the high priest said, "Do not bear false witness,[D] but tell the truth. You have stolen your wedding rights[E] and have not revealed it to the children of Israel. [17]And you have not lowered your head under the mighty hand in order that your offspring might be blessed."[F] [18]And Joseph was silent.

16 (1) [1]And the high priest said, "Give back the virgin[G] you received from the temple of the Lord." [2]And Joseph burst into tears. . .[H] [3]And the high priest said, "I will have you drink the

A. *the high priest said, "Joseph":* ὁ ἀρχιερεύς · Ἰωσήφ, so de Strycker (from P. Bodmer V). Tischendorf has ὁ ἱερεύς πρὸς Ἰωσήφ ("the priest said to Joseph"). P. Ashmolean lacks the conversation between the high priest and Joseph.

B. *As the Lord my God lives:* see note on 15:13 above. This time, however, it is Joseph's vow that is ineffective.

C. *As the Lord my God lives . . . witness of his truth:* ζῆ Κύριος ὁ Θεός μου καὶ ζῆ ὁ Χριστὸς αὐτοῦ καὶ ὁ τῆς ἀληθείας αὐτοῦ μάρτυς, so de Strycker. Tischendorf and P. Bodmer V have only ζῆ Κύριος ὁ Θεός (ζῆ Κύριος in Tischendorf). On de Strycker's reading see *La forme la plus ancienne,* 137 n.7 where he argues for an ancient trinitarian formula which was ultimately changed because it was misunderstood. De Strycker points to *1 Clem.* 58.2 and *Ascen. Isa. 3:13* for support of this possible early trinitarian reference.

D. *Do not bear false witness:* the harsh accusation against Joseph that he is lying is more serious given Joseph makes the declaration under oath.

E. *wedding rights:* γάμους σου, so de Strycker. In Tischendorf and P. Bodmer V the wedding rights belong to Mary: γάμους αὐτῆς.

F. *your offspring might be blessed:* the initial three-fold listing of Joseph's transgression by Annas the scribe increases to four when the high priest directly questions Joseph. The additional complaint is most curious in that it involves receiving blessings for Mary's child, something that has readily and consistently been established early on in the narrative—Mary and her child are indeed holy.

G. *Give back the virgin:* it is unclear to where Mary should be returned. While the temple from which she was asked to leave is surely not the high priest's intention, his response may serve to highlight Mary's closeness to the priesthood and the temple since it is a reminder that she once belonged there. The contradictions inherent in the high priests' indictment of Mary's virginal state while continuing to refer to her as a Virgin of the Lord reinforce the oddity of the questioning, but also afford Mary the opportunity to overcome another public testing of her purity and innocence.

H. *Joseph burst into tears:* περιδάκρυτος γενόμενος ὁ Ἰωσήφ. De Strycker

Lord's water of conviction,^A and it will reveal your sin before your own eyes."^B

cf. Num 5:11–31

(2) ⁴And the high priest took (the water) and made Joseph drink it and sent him away into the wilderness,^C but he came back whole. ⁵And then he made the child (Mary)^D drink it and also sent her away into the wilderness,^E but she too came back whole. ⁶And all the people were amazed^F because their sin was not revealed.

(*La forme la plus ancienne*, 137) suspects that the text is corrupt here since the main verb is missing in both P. Bodmer V and other manuscripts (i.e., rendered literally, the sentence reads "Joseph, bursting into tears").

A. *Lord's water of conviction*: the Lord's drink test recalls the bitter water test of Num 5:11–31, in which a test is administered to a woman and used as a type of abortive device to punish and reveal her illegitimate pregnancy. As discussed in the Introduction, this detail is often used to question the text's relationship with Judaism since the details of the test conducted in the *Protevangelium* do not line up with those found in Numbers. When the test is administered in the *Protevangelium*, both Mary and Joseph are required to drink with the purpose of disclosing their sin, not to determine an illegitimate child. As a truth-telling serum, the detail of the bitter water test has closer affinities to the suspected adulteress scene in Mishnah *Sotah*. In contrast to Mary's first testing and confrontation with Joseph, this testing by a physical ordeal undergone by both Mary and Joseph is extremely public and witnessed not only by the priests but also by the people (16:6).

B. *reveal your sin before your own eyes*: the drink test as explained by the high priest is curious in that it is supposed to reveal to Mary and Joseph their own sin, something they are both convinced is false. Unlike the first questioning of Mary when Joseph suspects she has transgressed, this public testing is heightened in intensity because it involves the priests and people of Israel, requires proving their innocence physically, and includes a charge that is explicitly couched in language involving sin. The questioning is not simply about whether Mary is sexually pure, but also whether she is guilty, which implies her possible involvement in an impurity that defiles morally.

C. *wilderness*: τὴν ἔρημον, here and in 16:5 so de Strycker (from P. Bodmer V). Tischendorf has τὴν ὀρεινήν ("the hill country").

D. *the child*: τὴν παῖδα, so de Strycker (from P. Bodmer V). Many of Tischendorf's manuscripts have "Mary," others have "the virgin" (παρθένον). De Strycker's chosen reading of "the child" highlights Mary's age and thus her irregular marriage arrangement.

E. *wilderness*: Joseph's and Mary's time in the wilderness recalls Joachim's stay in the wilderness at 1:9. Like Joachim, both return with good news.

F. *all the people were amazed*: given that the priests and people of Israel had confirmed Mary's purity earlier in the narrative, their surprise functions to heighten and reaffirm Mary's purity and innocence despite the obvious paradox of Mary's virginal yet visibly pregnant body. The people's confirmation of Mary's purity and innocence is yet another example of the string of

(3) [7]And the high priest said, "If the Lord God did not reveal your sin, then neither do I condemn you."[A] And he let them go. [8]And Joseph took Mary[B] and returned home,[C] rejoicing and praising the God of Israel.

cf. John 8:10

17 (1) [1]Now an order came out from King Augustus[D] that everyone in Bethlehem of Judea be registered for a census.[E] [2]And Joseph said, "I will register my sons, but what shall I do with this child?[F] How shall I register her? [3]As my wife? I'm too ashamed to do that. As my daughter? The children of Israel know that she is not my daughter. [4]On this day of the Lord, he will do as he wishes."[G]

cf. Luke 2:1–4

---

public declarations of Mary's special and blessed status.

A. *neither do I condemn you:* the high priest's words recall Jesus' words to the woman caught in adultery in John 8:10.

B. *Mary:* Μαριάμμην, so de Strycker (from P. Bodmer V). Tischendorf has Μαριάμ.

C. *returned home:* Joseph's active taking of Mary and returning home reinforces his sincere change of heart and decision to protect her at 14:8.

D. *King Augustus:* some translators have chosen emperor for historical accuracy since Augustus ruled not just a kingdom, but an empire. Additionally, Augustus was referred to as *imperator* not *rex.*

E. *registered for a census:* in Luke, Augustus's orders involve the enrollment of the entire world, whereas the decree is limited here to simply Bethlehem.

F. *I will register my sons, but what shall I do with this child:* this addition to Luke provides two details that reinforce Joseph's and Mary's unusual relationship. First, the reference to Joseph's son recalls Joseph's two-point protest for taking on Mary (9:8): he is old and already has children from a previous marriage. Second, Joseph's repeated reference to Mary as "child" highlights his role as her protector rather than traditional husband. Additionally, the explicit reference to Joseph's sons seems to support the stance of Epiphanius (*Pan.* 78.8.1; 78.9.6) on the controversial issue of Jesus' siblings raised by Mark 6:3 and Matt 13:56, since they are attributed to Joseph from a previous marriage; curiously though, no references to Jesus' sisters are made. In *Hist. Jos. Carp.* 2, Joseph also identifies four sons but also two daughters: Lysia and Lydia.

G. *as he wishes:* βούλεται, so de Strycker (from P. Bodmer V). Tischendorf specifies Κύριος as the subject ("do as the Lord wishes").

(2) ⁵And he saddled his donkey^A and sat her on it; and his son^B led it while Samuel^C followed behind. ⁶As they approached the third mile, Joseph turned around and saw that she was sad. ⁷And he said to himself,^D "Maybe the child in her is causing her uneasiness." ⁸Then Joseph turned around again and saw her laughing and said to her, "Mary,^E why is it that I see your face laughing one moment, but then sad another moment?" ⁹And she replied,^F "Joseph, because my eyes see two peoples^G: one lamenting and mourning and the other one cheerful and rejoicing."

A. *donkey:* no reference to a donkey is cited in Luke despite its common appearance in pictorial art on the "Christmas story." This familiar detail has its origins in this apocryphal text.

B. *his son:* two sons accompany Joseph and Mary on their trip; the first of these two sons is unidentified, the other is named Samuel (see note on 17:5 below). Some have suggested that the unidentified son may be a reference to the author himself. If this is the case, James, the self-identified author at 25:1, would be an eyewitness to the events he purports to record (Hock, *Infancy Gospels*, 63; Smid, *Protevangelium Jacobi*, 120). In the Armenian versions, one of Joseph's sons, identified as Manuel, accompanies Mary on the trip (17.2; ed. Terian).

C. *Samuel:* Samuel, James, and Simon are all attested in the manuscript tradition as names of the character here. Cf. Mark 6:3 and Matt 13:55, which propose the names James and Simon (though not Samuel), as brothers of Jesus. Tischendorf's text has Joseph following behind. Given the double reference to Joseph "turning around" (17:6 and 17:8) to see Mary the notion that Joseph is behind the caravan is problematic (Hock, *Infancy Gospel*, 63 n. 17:5).

D. *he said to himself:* καὶ εἶπεν ἐν ἑαυτῷ, so Tischendorf. De Strycker (from P. Bodmer V) has καὶ ἔλεγεν but the context seems to indicate that Joseph poses this question to himself.

E. *Mary:* see note on 16:8 above.

F. *she replied:* Mary speaks only eight times in five different scenes throughout the narrative. The first scene involves her questioning twice how she will conceive and give birth (11:6 and 11:9). The second scene involves Mary questioning aloud why all the generations will congratulate her since she has forgotten her conversation with the angel Gabriel (12:6). Mary offers two emphatic declarations of her innocence and purity in a third scene against Joseph who accuses her otherwise (13:8 and 13:10). Mary repeats her innocence and purity when she is required to defend herself again, but this time it is before the high priest (15:13). In the fifth and final scene, Mary's direct voice speaks prophetically about her unborn son's role in the world as savior and by association, her role as the mother of the Lord (17:9) before she instructs Joseph to help her down from the donkey (17:10).

G. *my eyes see two peoples:* the meaning of Mary's response to Joseph is

(3) [10]And when they came to the halfway point, Mary[A] said to him, "Joseph, take me down from the donkey because the child inside me is pressing his weight on me to come forth." [11]And he took her down from there and said to her, "Where can I take you to hide your shameful nakedness[B] because this place is wilderness."[C]

---

unclear. Simeon's prophecy in Luke 2:34 of the child "destined for the falling and rising of many in Israel" has elements in common, but here the prophetic words are placed on the lips of Mary. The specific reference to two peoples may also have resonance with Rebecca's pregnancy with her twin boys (Esau and Jacob) who are described by the Lord as being two nations or two peoples divided (Gen 25:23). Other interpretations include Jesus' ultimate sacrifice for the sins of all people, which evokes grief for Mary for the death of her son on the one hand, but also great joy on the other, because her son will be responsible for the salvation of humanity. One further interpretation identifies the two peoples as the rise of the believers (i.e., "Gentiles" and "Christianity") and the fall of unbelievers (i.e., "Jews" and "Judaism") (see van Stempvoort, "Protevangelium Jacobi," 421–22).

A. *Mary:* see note on 16:8 above.

B. *your shameful nakedness:* σου τὴν ἀσχημοσύνην. The idea is to provide her with privacy and protection.

C. *wilderness:* wilderness appears several times throughout the narrative. While it often denotes an unstable and undesirable locale, it has produced positive results for the characters in the narrative: when Joachim heads to the wilderness to punish himself, he returns redeemed and is given the good news of his wife's pregnancy; when Joseph and Mary are sent to the wilderness because they are accused of transgressions, they both return vindicated. Now the wilderness is marked as the location of Jesus' birth.

18 (1) ¹He found a cave^A there and took her inside it. And he positioned his sons^B to guard her ²and went out to search for a Hebrew midwife^C in the area around Bethlehem.^D

A. *He found a cave:* instead of a manger or inn (Luke 2:7) or a house (Matt 2:11), the *Protevangelium* uniquely locates the birth of Jesus in a cave in the wilderness, at a halfway point to their destination. See *Hist. Jos. Carp.* 7, which describes this locale as near the tomb of Rachel. To be sure, caves as birth locations are popularly found in Greek and Roman literature and often are connected to the births of gods and heroes (e.g., Zeus, Hermes, etc.), thus linking Jesus' birthplace to his divine nature. Justin Martyr (*Dial.* 78.5) attests to Jesus' birth in a cave, after having failed to secure lodging in Bethlehem, but also to the visit of the Arabian magi. So too is Jesus' birth in a cave attested by Origen (*Cels.* 1.51), who adds that "even among the enemies of our faith it is being said that in this cave Jesus was born." Although lost to tradition in Western Christendom, the detail of the cave has been so popular that even to this day it determines Eastern Christian art and celebrations of the Nativity (Shoemaker, *Mary in Early Christian Faith*, 49). Later traditions hold that the cave in which Jesus is born is also the burial place for Eve. This tradition connects to versions that hold Calvary as the locale where both Jesus dies and Adam is buried. See Stone, "Bones of Adam and Eve," 241–45.

B. *he positioned his sons:* if the unidentified son is indeed James, both he and his brother stand as eyewitnesses to the birth of Jesus. Note too that this scene contrasts sharply with Joseph's earlier departure when he leaves Mary in God's protection (9:12); Joseph now ensures that Mary is provided with physical protection.

C. *Hebrew midwife:* cf. Exod 2:7 for the reputation of Hebrew midwives.

D. *area around Bethlehem:* while the narrator notes that they are in the wilderness, it is not so far out that it prevents Joseph from being able to walk quickly to a more developed area to locate a Hebrew midwife.

(2) ³And I, Joseph,ᴬ was walking, and yet I was not walking.ᴮ ⁴And I looked up to the vault of heavenᶜ and saw it standing still,ᴰ and to the air and saw it seized in amazement,ᴱ and the birds of the sky were at rest. ⁵And I looked down to the earth and I

A. *And I, Joseph . . . everything returned to its course* (18:3–11): both the shift in content and the shift to the first person marks this section as distinct from the rest of the text. P. Bodmer V offers a much shorter version of 18:1—19:11, 20:1–7, and 21:3–10, and in fact, along with two other manuscripts (Vatican, Biblioteca Apostolica Vaticana, Vat. gr. 455 and Vat. gr. 654) actually omits completely the Joseph vision. See also London, British Library, Add. 14484 (Syriac; 6th cent.), an early reception of the text, which reduces the entire Joseph vision to two lines: "But I, Joseph was walking about, and I saw everything as though astonished; and suddenly everything loosened and ran on its proper order." Given that this section is likely to be older than the P. Bodmer V version and belonged to the original text, it is included here as reconstructed by de Strycker (*La forme la plus ancienne*, 147–51). Joseph's vision, which involves his seeing everything suspended in time, is used to signify the exact moment Jesus enters into the world. Joseph's physical separation from the birth parallels his necessary physical separation from Mary during her conception, but also offers meaning to the extraordinary event: the freezing of nature and of the activities of humans and animals underscores the significance of the birth. In this way, the cloud that overshadows the cave the moment Jesus enters into the world corresponds to the moment time is suspended (see Bovon, "Suspension of Time," 393–405). Nature's response to defining cosmic events also occurs with Jesus' death when the moment is marked by complete darkness, the tearing of the temple curtain, earthquakes, and the splitting of rocks (Matt 27:45–51). See also Rev 8:1 where roughly a half an hour of silence ensues after the Lamb opens up the seventh seal.

B. *yet I was not walking:* the first person voice of Joseph may be used to authenticate the events unfolding before him, but the reference to Joseph also not being able to walk suggests that he is not simply observing but participating in the suspension of time, although he is not completely frozen since he describes being able to look upwards and beyond (Bovon, "Suspension of Time," 400–401 and Smid, *Protevangelium Jacobi*, 128–30).

C. *to the vault of heaven:* εἰς τὸν πόλον τοῦ οὐρανοῦ, so de Strycker. Tischendorf has εἰς τὸν ἀέρα ("to the air").

D. *saw it standing still:* εἶδον αὐτὸν ἑστῶτα, so de Strycker. Tischendorf has εἶδον τὸν ἀέρα ἔκθαμβον ("saw the air seized in amazement").

E. *I saw the air seized in amazement:* εἰς τὸν ἀέρα καὶ εἶδον αὐτὸν ἔκθαμβον, so de Strycker. Tischendorf has ἀνέβλεψα εἰς τὸν πόλον τοῦ οὐρανοῦ, καὶ εἶδον αὐτὸν ἑστῶτα ("I looked up to the vault of heaven and saw it standing still"). The single word ἔκθαμβος is used to capture the moment of awe evoked from experiencing this event, though its complete meaning in this context is unclear. Immobilization and awe are the response of the world to the moment God intervenes and acts (Bovon, "Suspension of Time," 403).

saw a bowl laid there and workers reclining around it[A] with their hands in the bowl. [6]But the ones chewing were not chewing; and the ones lifting up something to eat were not lifting it up; and the ones putting food in their mouths were not putting food into their mouths. [7]But all their faces were looking upward;[B] [8]And I saw sheep being driven along,[C] but the sheep stood still. [9]And the shepherd raised his hand to strike them with a rod,[D] but his hand was still raised. [10]And I looked down upon the flowing river and I saw some young goats with their mouths over the water[E] but they were not drinking.[11]Then all at once everything returned to its course.

19 (1) [1]And I saw[F] a woman coming down from the hill country and she said to me, "Man, where are you going?" [2]I replied, "I am searching for a Hebrew midwife."[G] [3]And she asked me, "Are you from Israel?" [4]And I said to her, "Yes."[5]And she asked, "Then who is the one who has given birth in a cave?" [6]And I replied, "My betrothed." [7]And she said to me, "Is she not your wife?" [8]And I

A. *workers lying around it*: along with the descriptions at 8:9, this detail has parallels with Luke 2:8, which describes angels appearing to shepherds while guarding their flock in the open night air (Bovon, "Suspension of Time," 403).

B. *looking upward*: κατανευόντα ("nodding" or "looking downward") is attested in some manuscripts; ἄνω βλέποντα is the preferred and more sensible reading since the development of the text seems to indicate an upward movement towards the heavens.

C. *I saw sheep being driven along*: εἶδον ἐλαυνόμενα πρόβατα, so de Strycker. Tischendorf has ἰδοὺ πρόβατα ἐλαυνόμενα ("behold, sheep were being driven along").

D. *with a rod*: lacking in Tischendorf.

E. *the water*: lacking in Tischendorf.

F. *And I saw . . . Come and see* (19:1–11): while the suspension of time breaks at 18:11 with the return of nature to its normal state, Joseph continues to speak in the first person and partakes in a conversation with a woman who agrees to help Mary with the delivery after questioning him about their relationship. P. Bodmer V offers a significantly shorter version of the entire exchange with the midwife, reading only, "It is Mary, my betrothed, but she conceived by the Holy Spirit after she was raised in the temple of the Lord."

G. *Hebrew midwife*: the distinguishing feature that the midwife is Jewish may speak to the continued concern to ensure that Jesus' birth is accomplished with someone familiar with proper rites and regulations associated with childbirth.

replied to her, "She is Mary, the one who was brought up^A in the temple of the Lord; and I received her by lot as my wife. ⁹But she is not my wife; however, she has conceived by the Holy Spirit."^B ¹⁰And the midwife said, "Is this true?" ¹¹And Joseph said to her,^C "Come and see." ¹²And the midwife went with him.

(2) ¹³And they stood in front of^D the cave.^E And a dark cloud^F overshadowed the cave. ¹⁴And the midwife said, "My soul has

A. *brought up*: ἀνατραφεῖσα. Some manuscripts add εἰς τὰ ἅγια τῶν ἁγίων ("in the Holy of Holies").

B. *Then who is . . . But she is not my wife* (19:5–9): in Joseph's awkward and cumbersome explanation of his relationship with Mary, he refers to her as his "wife," "betrothed," and "not really his wife," almost in a single breath. His hesitancy or inability to concretely confirm their relationship reinforces the continued theme of his role as Mary's protector rather than traditional husband.

C. *Joseph said to her*: Joseph's concluding remarks return to the third person when he instructs her to follow him to see for herself the miracle of the virgin birth.

D. *in front of*: in the Syriac manuscript London, British Library, Add. 14484, Joseph and the midwife are *in* the cave rather simply *in front of* or *at the entrance of* the cave.

E. *cave*: Mary's exceptional purity is also reinforced with the location of the cave. Out in the wilderness, the cave stands as potentially offering the most danger, but Mary's extreme purity, especially in her role as the Lord's Virgin, allows the cave to be transformed into the safest of spaces so that even the son of God can be born and fed immediately by virgin milk. The isolation of the cave's location also reinforces the idea that Mary will need no assistance with the delivery since she is too far from civilization and the likelihood of finding help are slim. Even when Joseph successfully locates a midwife, they are too late to help with the actual delivery.

F. *dark cloud*: νεφέλη σκοτεινή, so de Strycker (from P. Bodmer V). Tischendorf has νεφέλη φωτεινή ("bright cloud"). The "dark cloud" may have been influenced by the manifestation of God as a dark cloud esp. in Exod 19:16–18 (de Strycker, *La forme la plus ancienne*, 155 n.4; Hock, *Infancy Gospels*, 67). Those who have opted for a "bright cloud" do so on the basis of a connection with Exod 16:10 and Num 16:42 (Daniels, *Manuscript Tradition*, 2.769; Smid, *Protevangelium Jacobi*, 134–38). The theophany where God is described as a cloud in general is also found, e.g., in Exod 13:21–22; 14:19, 24; 16:10; and 33:9–10. The cloud may also recall the angel's description of the conception at the annunciation: "the power of God will overshadow you" (11:7; so Foskett, *Virgin Conceived*, 159) as well as the marking of sacred space as seen in Exod 40:35 where Moses is unable to access the tabernacle because "the cloud covered the tent of meeting and the glory of God filled the tabernacle." Like Moses, who must wait until the tent is no longer filled with the glory of God to enter, Joseph and the midwife must wait until the cloud recedes

been magnified today because my eyes have seen an incredible
cf. Luke 2:30, 32 sign; for salvation has been born to Israel."ᴬ ¹⁵And immediately
the cloud contracted from the cave and a great lightᴮ appeared
within the cave so that their eyesᶜ could not bear it. ¹⁶A little time
afterwards that light began to contract until an infantᴰ could be
seen. And he came and took the breast of his mother,ᴱ Mary.

¹⁷And the midwife cried out and said, "How great is this day
for me, for I have seen this wondrous sight."ᶠ

(Vanden Eykel, *Looking Up*, 145).

A. *salvation has been born to Israel:* in Luke 2:30, 32 these words are spoken by Simeon. Note too that Simeon explicitly includes the gentiles in this
salvation, whereas the midwife does not.

B. *great light:* the theophanic language of the light continues from the
dark cloud that first hovers over the cave at 19:13. The great light acutely
marks the exact moment Jesus enters the world.

C. *their eyes:* several manuscripts have the first person plural so that
instead of "their eyes," "our eyes" is attested, bringing the witnessing of the
event shared additionally by the other sons who were instructed to stand
watch.

D. *infant:* while the finding of a midwife by Joseph is seemingly in vain
given that the child is already born upon their arrival, she perhaps provides
an even more significant role as witness to the miraculous birth. The generally hasty manner in which Mary gives birth may recall the story about the
conversation between Pharaoh and the midwives in Exod 1:19. When Pharaoh questions the midwives as to why they have not killed the male children
as instructed, they respond by saying that "Hebrew women are not like Egyptian women; for they are vigorous and give birth before the midwife comes
to them." Midwives clearly function as an important part in the narrative of
Jesus' birth, but the help they provide is not based on their skills as midwives.

E. *took the breast of his mother:* cf. 5:9–10 recalling Anna's feeding of
Mary earlier. The difference, however, is that Anna, in accordance with Lev
12:26 (which equates the ritual impurity of a new mother with that of a menstruant), interprets her condition as a new mother as ritually defiling so that a
prescribed time and proper cleansing is required before she can nurse Mary.
In this way, Anna's actions suggest her belief in the contagion potential of a
parturient to a newborn even through breastmilk, an extreme interpretation
that is not supported in biblical or rabbinical writings. The idea that a parturient's impurity is transferable to an infant, however, is attested in the *Damascus Document* (4Q266 6 ii 11) where a wet-nurse is required because it is
explicitly forbidden for a new mother to nurse her child until the prescribed
days are fulfilled. Mary's immediate nursing of her child, in contrast to her
own mother, is a clear statement of her extraordinary position and purity.

F. *I have seen this wondrous sight:* the midwife's humble response (along
with Salome's eventual declaration of belief at 20:10) to seeing the miracle

(3) [18]And the midwife went out of the cave and met Salome[A] and said to her, "Salome, Salome, I have a wondrous sight to tell you about: a virgin has given birth,[B] something that is contrary to her physical nature."[C] [19]And Salome said, "As the Lord my

cf. Isa 7:14

---

and her role as witness to the events is distinguishable from Matthew's and Luke's version of the infancy, which privilege men (magi and shepherds) as first recipients of the news.

A. *Salome*: there is no clear indication from where the name or character of Salome derived, and like Elizabeth (12:3), she is not introduced in the narrative, but suddenly appears. Mark 15:41 makes reference to a certain Salome who, along with Mary Magdalene and Mary the mother of James the Younger and Joses, was at the crucifixion. The infamous daughter of Herodias is also named Salome, but there are few connections between her character and the mid-wife Salome (Mark 6:17–28; Matt 14:6–11). While it is not clear precisely who Salome is or why she happens to come across the cave wherein Jesus is born, she functions to confirm and witness Mary's virginal status after the birth of Jesus, but also to serve as an antithetical character to the eager-to-believe midwife, since unlike the midwife, Salome requires physical proof to believe.

B. *a virgin has given birth*: the incredible paradox of Mary's new status as a virgin and mother requires the confirmation of several more witnesses. While the unnamed midwife unequivocally declares her belief in the miracle, the arrival of the Salome character functions as a foil to further substantiate the claim that the impossible has been made possible.

C. *contrary to her physical nature*: while the questioning of a virgin giving birth may first involve questioning whether her condition has been altered during conception, the focus on the birth itself poses the question of whether Mary was able to vaginally deliver an infant without any damage to her physical condition. In other words, virginal status can be altered not only by the intrusion that results from conception, but also by the intrusion caused by childbirth; the intrusion, whether it is going in or out, is equally damaging. Contrary to other births, Mary seems to show no signs of pain or blood. *her physical nature*: ἡ φύσις αὐτῆς. Some manuscripts have ἡ φύσις ἀνθρωπίνη ("human physical nature").

cf. John 20:25 God lives, unless I insert my finger[A] and examine her physical condition,[B] I will not believe that the virgin has given birth."

20 (1) ¹The midwife entered[C] and said, "Mary, ready yourself. For there is no small contention[D] concerning you." ²And when Mary heard this, she made herself ready.[E] And Salome inserted her finger into her to test her physical condition.[F]

A. *unless I insert my finger:* the description of Salome "inserting her fingers" parallels Thomas's insistence that he must also "insert his finger" into the mark of the nails left on Jesus' hands after the crucifixion in order to believe it is truly him (John 20:25). Like doubting Thomas, doubting Salome's disbelief is followed by complete conviction of Mary's paradoxical nature. Unlike Thomas, however, Salome's testing is logistically different. Whereas Thomas is invited to probe an open hole in order to believe, Salome's fingers are unable to probe an orifice that is surely closed. Moreover, Thomas does not actually insert his finger and hand into Jesus' hand and side—the appearance of Jesus and his reprimanding of Thomas's need to believe is what causes Thomas to believe. Salome's belief, on the other hand, is dependent upon her attempt at inserting her fingers into Mary's holy and untouchable virgin body; when Mary's body reacts violently to the intrusion, it is Salome's enflamed hand that convinces her to believe.

B. *physical condition:* φυσις (literally "nature"), in this context is more accurately translated as "genitalia," "vagina," or "vulva" (Foskett, *Virgin Conceived,* 159). These terms are more commonly used in writings among physicians, pharmacists, and farmers, etc. By contrast, they are seldom used in literature outside such professions.

C. *midwife entered . . . my payment from you* (20:1–7): the section on Salome's examination of Mary is heavily abbreviated in P. Bodmer V: "And she entered and made her ready. And Salome examined her condition. And Salome exclaimed that she had tempted the living God, 'And behold, my hand is (consumed) by fire, detaching itself from me.' And she prayed to the Lord and the midwife was cured at that same hour. And behold, an angel of the Lord appeared before Salome, saying, 'Your prayer has been heard before the Lord God. Come near and touch the child, and he will be your salvation.' And when she did so, Salome was cured; worshipping accordingly, she went forth from the cave. And behold, a voice of the angel of the Lord, saying . . ."

D. *no small contention:* the ordeal Mary is about to face resembles the two other tests she confronted and overcame; thus they prepared her (and the reader) to expect a similar outcome with this final and most challenging test.

E. *And when Mary heard this, she made herself ready:* so de Strycker. Lacking in Tischendorf.

F. *inserted her finger . . . to test:* this third testing (literally "ordeal") of Mary surpasses the other two tests she endures to defend her status as virgin (cf. her questioning by Joseph; her testing by the high priest) in that she must offer physical proof of her virginity by means of a gynecological

³And Salome cried out and said, "Woe for my lawlessness and for my disbelief;ᴬ for I have tested the living God.ᴮ ⁴And behold, my hand is on fire and falling awayᶜ from me."

(2) ⁵And she knelt before the Master, saying, "O God of my fathers, remember me because I am an offspring of Abraham, Isaac, and Jacob.ᴰ ⁶Do not make me an example to the children of Israel, but place me among the poor.ᴱ ⁷For you know, Master,

---

examination. Note that Mary's sexual status as pure is confirmed not by the physical anatomy of virginity but by the divine intervention of God in the form of punishment—Salome's hand becomes engulfed in fire. The *Protevangelium* clearly places value on the importance of physical and anatomical evidence to determine virginity even as it does not actually provide such evidence to confirm Mary's sexual virginity (Rosenberg, *Signs of Virginity*, 97–99). Cf. London, British Library, Add. 14484: "And she (Salome) drew near and saw that she was a virgin." While it is unclear precisely what Salome "saw," it nevertheless confirmed Mary's virginity for her. It is only after seeing and confirming Mary's virginity that Salome is punished for performing the examination.

A. *lawlessness . . . disbelief*: ἀνομία . . . ἀπιστία. Variant readings include: ἁμαρτία . . . ἀπιστία ("sin. . .disbelief") and ἀνομία . . . ἁμαρτία ("lawlessness . . . sin").

B. *I have tested the living God*: when Salome is punished, her offense involves disbelief via the testing of God. As expected, testing is a one way street—it is quite acceptable for God to test the faith and loyalty of his people, but quite objectionable the other way around. Additionally, that one who doubts Mary is immediately accused of doubting God himself is made clear in the punishment of fire emanating from her body, as God's interaction with humans is commonly depicted as fire that burns and punishes (e.g., God's glory via fire and cloud; Exod 40:38).

C. *my hand is on fire and falling away*: cf. Exod 4, which recalls Moses' diseased hand but also a refiguring of the burning bush. Salome's attempt at violating the most sacred space results in a violent punishment. Engulfed in flames, Salome's hand may metaphorically represent the fires of hell, but it may also equally and literally evoke the "light" or heat of God's protection for his most honored virgin since God is called a "consuming fire" in Deut 4:24; 9:3; Heb 12:29. "Consuming Fire" and "Ethical Goodness" are generally held as the two prominent components of holiness in Jewish tradition (Harrington, *Purity Texts*, 12–13). With regard to the "Consuming Fire" or holiness, contact with impurity or imperfection produces violent responses. In this way, Mary's holy body reacts violently to Salome's impure hand in a manner likened to the violent incompatibility between holiness and impurity.

D. *Abraham, Isaac, and Jacob*: Salome's reference to the biblical patriarchs serves to show the Israelites as first witnesses to the birth of Jesus.

E. *place me among the poor*: Salome's desire to be returned to the poor indicates that despite her disbelief, she is still a pious woman who once devoted

I have completed services in your name^A and have received my payment from you."

(3) ⁸And behold, an angel of the Lord appeared,^B saying to her, "Salome, Salome, the Master of all has heard your prayer.^C ⁹Bring your hand to the child and pick him up^D and you will have salvation and joy."

(4) ¹⁰And Salome came^E to the child and lifted him up, saying, "I will worship him, for he has been born a great king to Israel."^F ¹¹And Salome was immediately healed and went forth from the cave justified. ¹²And behold a voice said, "Salome, Salome, do not report the incredible things you have seen until the child goes to Jerusalem."^G

cf. Luke 18:14

cf. Luke 2:22–38

---

herself to caring for the poor and deserves forgiveness (cf. Tabitha in Acts 9:36–46). There are, however, a number of variants of this verse. Some manuscripts include "restore me to my parents," "restore my hand," and "show me mercy" (de Strycker, *La forme la plus ancienne*, 162 n.7).

A. *services in your name*: the detail of Salome's past work and services in God's honor confirm two narrative goals: first, she is a pious Jewish woman who erred, but came to believe; and second, that she is qualified in her profession as a midwife so that her testing of Mary's body confirms an untainted state.

B. *appeared*: ἐπέστη, so Tischendorf. De Strycker (following P. Bodmer V) has ἔστη ("stood").

C. *the Master of all has heard your prayer*: ἐπήκουσεν ὁ πάντων Δεσπότης τῆς δεήσεώς σου, so de Strycker (from P. Bodmer V). Tischendorf has ἐπήκουσεν σου Κύριος ("the Lord has heard you").

D. *pick him up*: the idea that Jesus holds miraculous healing power, even as a newborn, is not an uncommon tradition and is found in a number of other apocryphal narratives that feature the miracles of Mary and her son Jesus (e.g., *Arabic Infancy Gospel* and the related East Syriac *History of the Virgin*). In these narratives, miracles are achieved simply by touching, holding, or breathing in Jesus' odor. These miraculous powers extend even to Jesus' clothes, swaddling bands, and even bath water.

E. *And Salome came*: καὶ προσῆλθε Σαλώμη, so Tischendorf. De Strycker has λαβοῦσα δὲ χαρὰν προσῆλθε Σαλώμη ("and Salome joyfully came").

F. *king to Israel*: the title recalls Matt 27:42 and Mark 15:32, where Jesus is also given this title, but it is in jest with the intention of mocking him at the crucifixion.

G. *child goes to Jerusalem*: in Luke, Jesus first appears in Jerusalem for his presentation at the temple and to offer proper sacrifices. Since Salome does not appear again in the narrative, the expectation is that she simply went to Jerusalem and did not make contact with Mary or her child again. Cf. *Hist. Jos. Carp.* 8, where Salome stays with the Holy family in Egypt for a year.

21 (1) ¹And behold, Joseph was preparing to go to Judea, but there was a great commotion in Bethlehem of Judea.ᴬ ²For magiᴮ came saying, "Where is the kingᶜ of the Jews? For we saw his star in the East and have come to worship him."

Matt 2:1–2

(2) ³When Herod heardᴰ (about their visit) he was troubled and he sent servants to the magi. ⁴Then he sent for the high priests and he questioned them in the praetorium,ᴱ saying to them, "What is written about the Messiah? Where is he to be born?" ⁵They replied, "In Bethlehem of Judea, for that is what is written."ᶠ

Matt 2:3–6

⁶Then he released them. ⁷And he questioned the magi (saying to them),"What sign did you see concerning the king who has been born?" ⁸And the magi replied, "We saw an incredibly brilliant star shining among these stars, (so bright) it dimmed themᴳ so that they could not be seen. Therefore, we knew that a king had been born for Israel, and we came to worship him." ⁹Then Herod re-

Matt 2:7

ᴀ. *Bethlehem of Judea*: the description of Joseph preparing to go from Bethlehem to Judea is often cited as a geographical blunder (since Bethlehem is in Judea) revealing the author's lack of Palestinian geographical knowledge and therefore justification for his identification as a non-Jew. Not all manuscripts attest to this error. Some scholars have also argued that the geography may not be as problematic as it first appears. See Introduction, pp. 17–18.

ᴮ. *magi*: the magi travel to Bethlehem to see the child. In Matt 2:1, the arrival of the magi occurs in Jerusalem instead.

ᴄ. *king*: βασιλεύς, so de Strycker (from P. Bodmer V). Tischendorf has τεχθεὶς βασιλεύς ("newborn king").

ᴅ. *When Herod heard . . . head of the child* (21:3–10): P. Bodmer V again abbreviates the Herod and magi scene starting the narrative as follows: "And when Herod heard (about) it, he was troubled, and sent servants. And he made them come, and they told him about the star. And behold, they saw stars in the East/at its rising and it guided them until they entered into the cave; and it stood over the head of the child."

ᴇ. *in the praetorium*: ἐν τῷ πραιτωρίῳ, so de Strycker. Lacking in Tischendorf.

ꜰ. *In Bethlehem of Judea, for that is what is written*: when Herod poses this same question in Matt 2:3, Scripture is quoted, albeit a modified Mic 5:2 with 2 Sam 5:2, as a response. Here the reference is merely made to "what is written" in general.

ɢ. *it dimmed them*: the motif of a single star outshining all the other stars appears as an important point of interest for Justin Martyr (*1 Apol.* 32.12; *Dial.* 106.4), Ignatius of Antioch (*Eph.* 19.2), and a mostly unknown apocryphal text called the *Revelation of the Magi* (4:3–5; see further, Landau, *Revelation of the Magi*).

plied, "Go and search for him, and if you find him, report to me,
cf. Matt 2:8 so that I may also go to worship him."

(3) [10]Then the magi left, and behold, the star they had seen in the East led them forward till they came to the cave;[A] and it stood over the head of the child.[B] [11]The magi saw him standing[C] with his mother, Mary,[D] and they took from their leather pouches
cf. Matt 2:9–11 gifts[E] of gold, frankincense-tree, and myrrh.[F]

(4) [12]And having been warned by an angelic messenger not
cf. Matt 2:12 to go into Judea, they returned to their home by another route.

22 (1) [1]When Herod realized[G] he had been tricked by the magi, he grew angry [2]and sent his assassins, saying to them, "Kill all the
cf. Matt 2:16–18 infants[H] two years old and younger."[I]

A. *cave*: much like Matt 2:9, the star is responsible for leading the magi to the infant, who here is born in a cave rather than in a house (Matt 2:10).

B. *head of the child*: ἐπὶ τὴν κεφαλὴν τοῦ παιδίου, so de Strycker (from P. Bodmer V). Tischendorf has ἐπὶ τὴν κεφαλὴν τοῦ σπηλαίου ("entrance of the cave").

C. *standing*: ἑστῶτα. Given his mother's exceptional abilities as an infant, it is possible that Jesus too displays superior physical abilities and is indeed able to stand as an infant, but the author may have intended simply to imply that he was with his mother at the magi's arrival (de Strycker, *La forme la plus ancienne*, 173; Hock, *Infancy Gospels*, 73 n. 21:11).

D. *with his mother, Mary*: some manuscripts add πεσόντες προσεκύνησαν αὐτῷ καὶ ("bowed down and worshipped him"). Others place "and they worshipped him" after "myrrh."

E. *gifts*: δῶρα, so de Strycker (from P. Bodmer V). Lacking in Tischendorf.

F. *gold, frankincense-tree, and myrrh*: the number of magi in both the *Protevangelium* and Matthew are not identified, but three gifts are listed, contributing to the tradition of three separate magi. See also the *T. Adam* 3:6, in which the three treasures taken out of paradise are also gold, frankincense, and myrrh.

G. *When Herod realized*: τότε Ἡρώδης ἰδών, so de Strycker (from P. Bodmer V). Tischendorf has γνοὺς δὲ Ἡρώδης ("when Herod knew").

H. *Kill all the infants*: in Matthew the order affects Jesus alone, whereas in the *Protevangelium* Herod's orders also directly have an impact on Elizabeth and her son John.

I. *two years old and younger*: some manuscripts add a reference to Bethlehem (τοὺς ἐν βηθλεὲμ καὶ ἐν πᾶσι τοῖς ὁρίοις αὐτῆς: "in Bethlehem and all its boundaries") and others add a time frame involving the sighting of the star: κατὰ τὸν χρόνον τοῦ φαινομένου ἀστέρος ὃν ἠκρίβωσε παρὰ τῶν μάγων ("in accordance with the time the star appeared, which he learned from the magi").

(2) ³When Mary heard the infants were being killed, ⁴she was scared and took her child and wrapped him in swaddling clothes and placed him in an ox-manger.ᴬ

cf. Luke 2:7

(3) ⁵But when Elizabeth heard that they were looking for John, she took him and went up into the hill-country ⁶and was searching for any place to hide him, but there was no hiding place. ⁷Then Elizabeth sighed deeply and said,ᴮ "Mountain of God, take me in,ᶜ a mother with her child." For Elizabeth was not strong enough to climb the mountain because she was faint-hearted.ᴰ ⁸And immediately the mountain split open and received her. And the mountain was shining a light on herᴱ ⁹because an angel of the Lord was with them, protecting them.

23 (1) ¹And Herod was searching for John, ²and he sent forth servants to the altarᶠ for Zechariah, saying to him, "Where have you hidden your son?" ³But he answered, telling them, "I am a minister of God, serving in his temple.ᴳ How would I know where my son is?"

A. *ox-manger*: the *Protevangelium* harmonizes Luke's reference to the ox-manger with Matthew's threat by Herod on Jesus' life. Some manuscripts leave out the detail of Mary hiding Jesus in an ox-manger and simply have the holy family depart for Egypt instead (Smid, *Protevangelium Jacobi*, 152–53).

B. *Elizabeth sighed deeply and said*: Tischendorf adds φωνῇ μεγάλῃ ("in a loud voice").

C. *take me in*: δέξαι με, from P. Bodmer V. Tischendorf and de Strycker follow the majority of the manuscripts with simply δέξαι ("take in").

D. *For Elizabeth . . . faint-hearted*: so de Strycker (from P. Bodmer V). Lacking in Tischendorf.

E. *on her*: αὐτῇ, so de Strycker (from P. Bodmer V) and Tischendorf. Some manuscripts have αὐτοῖς ("them") since Elizabeth is with John.

F. *to the altar*: ἐν τῷ θυσιαστηρίῳ, so de Strycker (from P. Bodmer V). Lacking in Tischendorf, but some of his manuscripts have εἰς τὸ θυσιαστήριον Κυρίου ("the Lord's altar"). At 10:9, Zechariah was made mute and replaced by a certain Samuel but here he has resumed his office and his speech is restored.

G. *serving in his temple*: this is the first reference to the temple and its priest since Mary and Joseph are vindicated after Mary's virginity and Joseph's innocence are tested (16:4–8). The temple and its priest return at the final scenes of the narrative, but note that the altar will soon be polluted and the temple made profane and unusable when Zechariah refuses to divulge the whereabouts of his son and is slaughtered.

(2) ⁴And the servants left and reported everything to Herodᴬ who became angry and said, "His son is going to rule over Israel." ⁵Then he sent his servants back to him to say,ᴮ "Tell me the truth, where is your son? Because you know that your blood is in my hand."ᶜ ⁶And the servants left and reported this to him.

(3) ⁷And in response, Zechariahᴰ said, "I am a witness of God.ᴱ Take my blood,ᶠ ⁸for the Master will receive my spirit because you are shedding innocent bloodᴳ at the entrance of the Lord's temple." ⁹And Zechariah was murdered at daybreak, but the children of Israel did not know thatᴴ he was murdered.

cf. Matt 23:35

cf. Luke 1:8–10 **24** (1) ¹At the hour of greeting,ᴵ the priests came out, but Zechariah did not meet and bless them as was customary. ²And so the priests stood waiting for Zechariah to welcome him kindly with prayer and praise for the Most High God.

(2) ³But when he did not come, everyone grew fearful. ⁴One of them, however, took courage and entered the sanctuaryᴶ and saw dried blood beside the altar of the Lord. ⁵And (he heard) a

---

A. *to Herod:* so Tischendorf. De Strycker simply has "to him." The variant reading is preferred for clarity.

B. *Then he sent his servants back to him to say:* so de Strycker (from P. Bodmer V). Lacking in Tischendorf.

C. *your blood is in my hand:* i.e., your life is in my hand.

D. *Zechariah:* so Tischendorf. De Strycker simply has "he said." The variant reading is preferred for clarity.

E. *I am a witness to God:* some manuscripts repeat here Zechariah's defense ("How would I know where my son is?").

F. *take my blood:* ἔχε μου τὸ αἷμα, so de Strycker (from P. Bodmer V). Tischendorf has εἰ ἐκχέις μου τὸ αἷμα ("if you take my blood").

G. *shedding innocent blood:* the prophet Zechariah's innocent blood is referenced when Jesus denounces the scribes and Pharisees.

H. *that:* ὅτι, so Tischendorf. De Strycker (following P. Bodmer V) has πῶς ("how").

I. *hour of greeting:* Zechariah who is described as a priest is depicted in Luke entering the sanctuary of the Lord to offer incense according to the customs of the priesthood. The whole assembly of the people (here replaced by the other priests) wait for him at a distance to greet him. The expectation is that on his return, he will bless them and recite the prayers of supplication and praise.

J. *the sanctuary:* εἰς τὸ ἁγίασμα, so de Strycker (from P. Bodmer V). Lacking in Tischendorf.

voice saying, "Zechariah has been murdered and his blood will not be wiped away until his avenger[A] comes." [6]When he heard these words he was frightened and went out and reported to the priests what he had seen and heard.[B]

(3) [7]And taking up courage, they entered and saw what had happened. [8]And the ceiling panels of the temple cried out[C] and they ripped their clothes from top to bottom [9]and they did not find his corpse,[D] but they found his blood turned into stone.[E] [10]They were afraid and went out and reported[F] that Zechariah had been murdered. [11]And all of the tribes of the people heard and mourned for him and lamented for three days and three nights.

cf. 1 Sam 30:12; 2 Kgs 2:17; Jonah 1:17; Matt 12:40

(4) [12]After three days, however, the priests deliberated whom to appoint to Zechariah's place[13] and the lot fell on Simeon;[G] [14]for this is the one who was revealed by the Holy Spirit that he would not see death until he should see the Christ in the flesh.

cf. Luke 2:25–26

A. *avenger:* the identity of the "avenger" is unknown, but the author may be drawing on the phrase "avenger of blood" used commonly in Numbers (e.g., 35:19, 21, 24, 25, 27) and Deuteronomy (19:6, 12; 32:43).

B. *seen and heard:* so de Strycker. Lacking in Tischendorf. Some manuscripts add ἠνέῳξεν δὲ τὰς πύλας τοῦ ναοῦ τοῦ Κυρίου ("and the gates of the temple of the Lord opened").

C. *ceiling panels of the temple cried out:* the anthropomorphic description of the temple can be interpreted as an extension of God's response to the death of Zechariah. More specifically, the defilement of God's house via the spilling of Zechariah's blood at the altar results in an immediate and dramatic reaction.

D. *they did not find his corpse:* the assumption is that the corpse was taken and buried in an unmarked site rather than a resurrection akin to Jesus.

E. *blood turned into stone:* while there are numerous references in which things (e.g., moon, water, sea, river, etc.) are turned into blood via divine will and power (e.g., Joel 2:13; Exod 4:9, 7:17–21; Ps 78:44, 105:29; Isa 15:9; Rev 6:12; 8:8; 16:3, 4; 11:6), the idea of blood turning into stone is unique to the *Protevangelium.* The intention may simply be that Zechariah's blood had congealed since so much time passed between his murder and when someone finally entered the temple to witness the death scene; however, given the number of miraculous and inexplicable details included throughout the narrative, the interpretation of a supernatural occurrence should not be so easily dismissed either.

F. *reported:* Tischendorf adds παντὶ τῷ λαῷ ("to all the people").

G. *Simeon:* in Luke, Simeon is similarly described but in the context of Jesus' presentation at the temple rather than as Zechariah's replacement. Divine intervention via lot is utilized several times throughout this narrative (see 9:7 and 10:7).

25 (1) ¹And I, James,ᴬ the one who wrote this account in Jerusalem when there was an uproarᴮ at the time of Herod'sᶜ death,ᴰ
²hid myself away in the wildernessᴱ until the uproar in Jerusalem
stopped. ³There, I praised the Masterᶠ who gave me the wisdom
to write this account.

cf. Matt 2:19–20

(2) ⁴Grace will be with all those who fear the Lord. Amen.

Birth of Mary. Apocalypse of James.ᴳ

A. *Now I, James:* the narrative once again transitions into the first person.
Unlike the transition at 18:3 where Joseph is identified as the first person
speaker, here the first person is the author of the text (see authorship in the
Introduction). While James's exact relationship to Jesus has been explained
in various ways by the early Church Fathers—i.e., as a stepbrother (son of
Joseph by a previous wife) or a cousin (Joseph's brother Cleopas's son) as
indicated by Eusebius; or a cousin via Mary, Cleopas's wife (the sister of the
Virgin Mary) as indicated by Jerome—there is a general assumption that this
certain James is the elder brother of the Lord (Mark 6:3; Matt 13:55; Acts
12:17; 15:13; 21:18; 1 Cor 15:7; Gal 1:19). As such, James here stands as a
witness to the events he supposedly narrates.

B. *uproar:* see Josephus, *B.J.* 2.1.1–3 [1–13], which describes the uproar
after Herod's death as the result of a conflict with the masses over his son
Archelaus's authority. Josephus attests to the slaughtering of approximately
3000 people in the temple as they were praying or offering their sacrifices
and to the rest of the masses who had dispersed to the nearby mountains
(2.1.3 [13]). James, our so-called author, claims he wrote this account under
these conditions.

C. *Herod's:* given the reference to the command to have children two
years old and under killed at 22:1–2 (cf. Matt 2:19), the Herod in question is
most likely Herod the Great (d. 4 BCE). Herod the Great's grandson, Herod
Agrippa I (d. 44 CE), is also a possibility given his involvement with the per-
secution of the church and the death of James, the brother of John, son of
Zebedee (Acts 12:1–2) (See Hock, *Infancy Gospels,* 77 n. 25:1).

D. *death:* some variants have πικρῷ θανάτῳ ("bitter death").

E. *wilderness:* the wilderness functions once again as a positive locale in
the narrative. James here too finds safety and protection within the confines
of the wilderness.

F. *Master:* Δεσπότην, so de Strycker (from P. Bodmer V). Tischendorf
has Δεσπότην Θεόν ("God, the Master"); some manuscripts have Δεσπότην
Χριστόν ("Christ, the Master").

G. *Birth of Mary. Apocalypse of James:* this double title, found in P. Bodmer V, is lacking in Tischendorf. P. Bodmer V concludes with a farewell:
"Peace to the writer and to the reader."

Bibliography

Texts and Translations

Amann, Émile. *Le Protévangile de Jacques et ses remaniements latins. Introduction, textes, traduction et commentaire.* Les apocryphes du Nouveau Testament. Paris: Letouzey et Ané, 1910.

Bingen, Jean. "Protévangile de Jacques, XIII–XV (P. Ashmolean inv. 9)." *Chronique d'Égypte* 80 (2005) 210–14.

Brock, Sebastian P., trans. *Bride of Light: Hymns on Mary from the Syriac Churches.* Mōrān Ethō series 6. Kottayam, 1994. New ed. Piscataway, NJ: Gorgias, 2010.

Cameron, Ron, ed. and trans. *The Other Gospels: Non-Canonical Gospel Texts.* Philadelphia: Westminster John Knox, 1982, 107–21.

Cowper, Benjamin Harris, trans. *The Apocryphal Gospels and Other Documents Relating to the History of Christ.* 7th ed. London: Nutt, 1910. (1–26)

Cullmann, Oscar, trans. "The Protevangelium of James." In *New Testament Apocrypha*, edited by Wilhelm Schneemelcher, 1:421–39. Translation editor R. McL. Wilson. 2 vols. Rev. ed. Louisville: Westminster John Knox, 1991–1993.

———. "The Protevangelium of James." In *New Testament Apocrypha*, edited by Edgar Hennecke and Wilhelm Schneemelcher, 1:374–88. Translation editor R. McL. Wilson. 2 vols. 3rd ed. London: Luttersworth, 1963.

Ehrman, Bart D., and Zlatko Pleše, eds. and trans. *The Apocryphal Gospels: Texts and Translations.* Oxford: Oxford University Press, 2011. (18–36)

Elliott, J. K., ed. *The Apocryphal New Testament: A Collection of Apocryphal Christian Literature in an English translation.* Oxford: Oxford University Press, 1993. (48–67).

Fabricius, Johann Albert, ed. *Codex Apocryphus Novi Testamenti.* 2 vols. Hamburg: Schiller, 1703. (1:66–125)

Frey, Albert, trans. "Protévangile de Jacques." In *Écrits apocryphes chrétiens*, vol. 1, edited by François Bovon and Pierre Geoltrain, 71–104. Bibliothèque de la Pléiade 442. Paris: Gallimard, 1997.

Grynaeus, Johann Jacob. *Monumenta S. Patrum Orthodoxographa, hoc est Theologiae sacrosanctae ac syncerioris fidei Doctores, numero circiter LXXXV.* Basel: Heinrich Petri, 1569.

Heroldus, Johannes. *Orthodoxographa Theologiae Sacrosanctae ac syncerioris fidei Doctores Numero LXXVI.* Basil: Heinrich Petri, 1555. (3–9)

Hock, Ronald F., trans. "The Infancy Gospel of James." In *The Complete Gospels*, edited by Robert J. Miller, 380–96. San Francisco: HarperCollins, 1994.

———, ed. and trans. *The Infancy Gospels of James and Thomas.* Santa Rosa, CA: Polebridge, 1995. (1–81)

Hone, William, ed. *The Apocryphal New Testament: Being All the Gospels, Epistles, and Other Pieces Now Extant, Attributed in the Four First Centuries to Jesus Christ, His Apostles, and Their Companions, and Not Included in the New Testament by Its Compilers. Translated From the Original Tongues, and Now First Collected into One Volume.* London: Ludgate Hill, 1820. (24–37)

James, M. R., trans. *The Apocryphal New Testament: Being the Apocryphal Gospels, Acts, Epistles, and Apocalypses, with Other Narratives and Fragments.* Oxford: Clarendon, 1924. Corrected ed., 1953. (38–49)

Jones, Jeremiah, trans. *A Full and New Method of Settling the Canonical Authority of the New Testament.* 3 vols. London: Clark and Hett, 1726–1727. 2nd ed. Oxford: Clarendon, 1798. (99–129)

Lightfoot, J. B. et al., ed. *Excluded Books of the New Testament.* London: Nash & Grayson, 1927. (27–48)

Meyer, Arnold, trans. "Protevangelium des Jakobus." In *Handbuch zu den Neutestamentlichen Apokryphen*, edited by Edgar Hennecke, 106–31. Tübingen: Mohr/Siebeck, 1904.

Neander, Michel, ed. *Catechesis Martini Lutheri parva graeco-latina.* Basel: Oporinum, 1564. (356–92)

Shoemaker, Stephen J., trans. *The Life of the Virgin.* Maximus the Confessor. New Haven: Yale University Press, 2012.

Smid, Harm R. *Protevangelium Jacobi: A Commentary.* Translated by G. E. Van Baaren-Pape. Apocrypha Novi Testamenti 1. Assen: Van Gorcum, 1965.

Strycker, Émile de. *La forme la plus ancienne du Protévangile de Jacques.* SH 33. Brussels: Société des Bollandistes, 1961. (439–73)

Terian, Abraham, ed. and trans. *The Armenian Gospel of the Infancy with Three Early Versions of the Protevangelium of James.* Oxford: Oxford University Press, 2008.

Testuz, Michel, ed. and trans. *Papyrus Bodmer V: Nativité de Marie.* Cologne-Geneva: Bibliotheca Bodmeriana, 1958.

Tischendorf, Constantine von, ed. *Evangelia Apocrypha.* 1953. 2nd ed. Leipzig: Avenarius & Mendelssohn, 1876. (1–49)

Vööbus, Arthur, ed. *The Didascalia Apostolorum in Syriac.* CSCO 401–402, 407–408, Syr. 175–76, 179–80. Leuven: Sécretariat du CorpusSCO, 1979.

Walker, Alexander, trans. *Apocryphal Gospels, Acts and Revelations.* Edinburgh: T. & T. Clark, 1870. (16–52)

Wayment, Thomas A., ed. *The Text of the New Testament Apocrypha (100–400 CE).* London: T. & T. Clark, 2013. (51–79)

Studies and Other Works

Allen, John L. "The 'Protevangelium of James' as an 'Historia': The Insufficiency of the 'Infancy Gospel' Category." In *Society of Biblical Literature Seminar Papers, 1991*, edited by Eugene H. Lovering, 508–17. SBLSP 30. Atlanta: Scholars, 1991.

Backus, Irena. "Guillaume Postel, Théodore Bibliander et le 'Protévangile de Jacques." *Apocrypha* 6 (1995) 7–65.

Beattie, Tina. "Mary in Patristic Theology." In *Mary: The Complete Resource*, edited by Sarah Jane Boss, 75–105. New York: Oxford University Press, 2007.

BeDuhn, Jason D. *The First New Testament: Marcion's Scriptural Canon*. Salem, OR: Polebridge, 2013.

———. "The Myth of Marcion as Redactor." *Annali di Storia dell' Esegesi* 29 (2012) 15–42.

Bouwsma, William J. *Concordia Mundi: The Career and Thought of Guillaume Postel 1510–1581*. Cambridge: Harvard University Press, 1957.

Bovon, François. "Beyond the Canonical and the Apocryphal Books, the Presence of a Third Category: The Books Useful for the Soul." *HTR* 105 (2012) 125–37.

———. "The Suspension of Time in Chapter 18 of Protevangelium of Jacobi." In *The Future of Early Christianity: Essays in Honour of Helmut Koester*, edited by Birger A. Pearson et al., 393–405. Minneapolis: Fortress, 1991.

———. "'Useful for the Soul': Christian Apocrypha and Christian Spirituality." In *The Oxford Handbook of Early Christian Apocrypha*, edited by Andrew Gregory and Christopher Tuckett, 185–95. Oxford: Oxford University Press, 2015.

Brown, Peter. *The Body and Society: Men, Women, and Sexual Renunciation in Early Christianity*. New York: Columbia University Press, 1988.

Buck, Fidelis. "Are the 'Ascension of Isaiah' and the 'Odes of Solomon' Witnesses to an Early Cult of Mary?" In *De primordiis cultus mariani. Acta Congressus Mariologici-Mariani in Lusitania anno 1967 celebrati*, 371–99. Rome: Pontifica Academia Mariana Internationalis, 1970.

Cartlidge, David R., and J. K. Elliott. *Art and the Christian Apocrypha*. London: Routledge, 2001.

Conrady, Ludwig. "Das Protevangelum Jacobi in neuer Beleuchtung." *TSK* 62 (1889) 728–84.

Cooper, Jerrold S. "Virginity in Mesopotamia." In *Sex and Gender in the Ancient Near East*. Volume 1 of *Proceedings of the 47th Rencontre Assyriologique Internationale*, edited by Simo Parpola and Robert M. Whiting, 1:91–112. CRRAI 47. Helsinki: The Neo-Assyrian Text Corpus Project, 2002.

Cothenet, Édouard. "Le Protévangile de Jacques: Origine, Genre et Signification d'un Premier Midrash Chrétien sur la Nativité de Marie." In *ANRW* II.25.6 (1988) 4252–69.

Daniels, Boyd Lee. "The Greek Manuscript Tradition of the Protevangelium Jacobi." PhD diss., Duke University, 1956.

Dinker, E. "Die ersten Petrusdarstellungen. Ein archäologischer Beitrag zur Geschichte des Petrusprimates." *Marburger Jahrbuch für Kunstwissenschaft* 11 (1939) 1–80.

Elliot, J. K. "Christian Apocrypha and the Developing Role of Mary." In *The Oxford Handbook of Early Christian Apocrypha*, edited by Andrew Gregory and Christopher Tuckett, 267–88. Oxford: Oxford University Press, 2015.

Evans, Helen C., and Brandie Ratliff, eds. *Byzantium and Islam: Age of Transition, 7th–9th Century*. New York: Metropolitan Museum of Art, 2012.

Foskett, Mary F. *A Virgin Conceived: Mary and Classical Representation of Virginity*. Indianapolis: Indiana University Press, 2002.

———. "Virginity as Purity in the *Protevangelium of James*." In *A Feminist Companion to Mariology*, edited by Amy-Jill Levine with Maria Mayo Robbins, 67–76. Cleveland: Pilgrim, 2005.

Foster, Paul. "The Protevangelium of James." In *The Non-Canonical Gospels*, edited by Paul Foster, 110–25. New York: T. & T. Clark, 2008.

Frymer-Kensky, Tikva. "The Strange Case of the Suspected Sotah: Numbers 5.11–31." *VT* 34 (1984) 11–26.

Gaventa, Beverly Roberts. *Mary: Glimpses of the Mother of Jesus.* Personalities of the New Testament. 1999. Reprint, Minneapolis: Fortress, 1999.

Geyer, Paulus, ed. *Itinera Hierosolymitana, Saeculi III–VIII.* CSEL 39. Prague: Tempsky, 1893.

Glancy, Jennifer A. *Corporeal Knowledge: Early Christian Bodies.* Oxford: Oxford University Press, 2010.

Grabar, André. *Early Christian Art: From the Rise of Christianity to the Death of Theodosius.* New York: Odyssey, 1968.

Harnack, Adolf von. *Geschichte der altchristlichen Literatur bis Eusebius.* 2 vols. 2nd ed. Leipzig: Hinrichs, 1897.

———. *Marcion and the New Testament: An Essay in the Early History of the Canon.* Chicago: University of Chicago Press, 1942.

Harrington, Hannah K. *The Purity Texts.* Companion to the Qumran Scrolls 5. London: T. & T. Clark, 2004.

Harris, William V. *Ancient Literacy.* Cambridge: Harvard University Press, 1989.

Hasan-Roken, Galit. *Web of Life: Folklore and Midrash in Rabbinic Literature.* Translated by Batya Stein. Stanford: Stanford University Press, 2000.

Hayes, Christine Elizabeth. *Gentile Impurities and Jewish Identities: Intermarriage and Conversion from the Bible to the Talmud.* Oxford: Oxford University Press, 2002.

Horner, Timothy. "Jewish Aspects of the Protevangelium of James." *JECS* 12 (2004) 313–35.

Hurtado, Larry W. "Who Read Early Christian Apocrypha?" In *The Oxford Handbook of Early Christian Apocrypha*, edited by Andrew Gregory and Christopher Tuckett, 153–66. Oxford: Oxford University Press, 2015.

Jensen, Robin M. "The Apocryphal Mary in Early Christian Art." In *The Oxford Handbook of Early Christian Apocrypha*, edited by Andrew Gregory and Christopher Tuckett, 289–305. Oxford: Oxford University Press, 2015.

Klauck, Hans-Josef. *Apocryphal Gospels: An Introduction.* Translated by Brian McNeil. London: T. & T. Clark, 2003.

Klawans, Jonathan. *Impurity and Sin in Ancient Judaism.* Oxford: Oxford University Press, 2000.

———. *Purity, Sacrifice, and the Temple: Symbolism and Supersessionism in the Study of Ancient Judaism.* Oxford: Oxford University Press, 2006.

Kraus, Thomas J., and Tobias Nicklas. *Das Petrusevangelium und die Petrusapokalypse: Die griechischen Fragmente mit deutscher und englischer Übersetzung.* GCS, N.F. 11. Berlin: de Gruyter, 2004.

Lafontaine-Dosogne, Jacqueline. *Iconographie de l'enfance de la Vierge dans l'Empire byzantin et en Occident.* 2 vols. Mémoires de la Classe des lettres. Collection in-4o; 2e sér., t. 11, fasc. 3-3b.. Brussels: Palais des Académies, 1964.

Liberman, Saul and Frédéric Manns. "Une Ancienne Tradition sur la Jeunesse de Marie." In *Essais sur le Judeo-Christianisme*, 106–14. SBFA 12. Jerusalem: Analecta, 1977.

Lowe, Malcolm. "ΙΟΥΔΑΙΟΙ of the Apocrypha: A Fresh Approach to the Gospels of James, Pseudo-Thomas, Peter and Nicodemus." *NovT* 23 (1981) 56–90.

Mach, Michael. "Are There Jewish Elements in the Protevangelium Jacobi?" In *Proceedings of the World Congress of Jewish Studies, Jerusalem, Aug. 1985*, 215–22. Jerusalem: World Union of Jewish Studies, 1986.

Minov, Sergey. "'Serpentine' Eve in Syriac Christian Literature of Late Antiquity." In *With Letters of Light: Studies in the Dead Sea Scrolls, Early Jewish Apocalypticism, Magic, and Mysticism in Honor of Rachel Elior*, edited by Daphna V. Arbel and Andrei A. Orlov, 92–114. Ekstasis 2. Berlin: de Gruyter, 2010.

Murray, Robert. "Mary, the Second Eve in the Early Syriac Fathers." *Eastern Churches Review* 3 (1971) 372–84.

Nicklas, Tobias. "The Influence of Jewish Scriptures On Early Christian Apocrypha." In *The Oxford Handbook of Early Christian Apocrypha*, edited by Andrew Gregory and Christopher Tuckett, 141–52. Oxford: Oxford University Press, 2015.

Nongbri, Brent. "Recent Progress in Understanding the Construction of the Bodmer 'Miscellaneous' or 'Composite' Codex." *Adamantius* 21 (2015) 171–72.

Norelli, Enrico, ed. *Ascensio Isaiae: Commentarius*. CCSA 8. Turnhout: Brepols, 1995.

———. *Ascension du prophète Isaïe*. Apocryphes: Collection de poche de l'AELAC. Turnhout: Brepols, 1993.

———. *L'Ascensione di Isaia: Studi su un apocrifo al crocevia dei cristianesimi*. Origini N.S. 1. Bologna: Centro editorial dehoniano, 1994.

———. *Marie des Apocryphes. Enquête sur la mère de Jésus dans le christianisme antique*. Christianismes Antiques 1. Geneva: Labor et Fides, 2009.

Peppard, Michael. *The World's Oldest Church: Bible, Art, and Ritual at Dura- Europos, Syria*. New Haven: Yale University Press, 2016.

Plumpe, Joseph C. "Some Little-Known Early Witnesses to Mary's Virginitas in Partu." *TS* 9 (1948) 567–77.

Pratscher, Wilhelm. *Der Herrenbruder Jakobus und die Jakobustraditionen*. FRLANT 139. Göttingen: Vandenhoeck & Ruprecht, 1987.

Raithel, Jutta C. "Beginning at the End: Literary Unity and the Relationship Between Anthropology and Liturgy in the *Protevangelium Jacobi* (*P. Bodm. 5*)." PhD diss., Catholic University of America, 2011.

Rosenberg, Michael. "Penetrating Words: A Babylonian Rabbinic Response to Syriac Mariology." *JJS* 67 (2016) 121–34.

———. "Sexual Serpents and Perpetual Virginity: Marian Rejectionism in the Babylonian Talmud." *JQR* 106 (2016) 465–93.

———. *Signs of Virginity: Testing Virgins and Making Men in Late Antiquity*. New York: Oxford University Press, 2018.

Roth, Dieter. *The Text of Marcion's Gospel*. NTTS 49. Leiden: Brill, 2015.

Satlow, Michael L. *Jewish Marriage in Antiquity*. Princeton: Princeton University Press, 2001.

Schiller, Gertrud. *Ikonographie der christlichen Kunst*. 5 vols. Gütersloh: Mohn, 1966–1991.

Schubert, Ursula "Die Kindheitsgeschichte Jesu als politische Theologie am Triumphbogenmosaik von Santa Maria Maggorie in Rom." In *Byzantine East, Latin West: Art Historical Studies in Honor of Kurt Weitzmann*, edited by Doula Mouriki, 81–89. Princeton: Princeton University Press, 1995.

Shoemaker, Stephen J. "Between Scripture and Tradition: The Marian Apocrypha of Early Christianity." In *The Reception and Interpretation of the Bible in Late Antiquity: Proceedings of the Montréal Colloquium in Honour of Charles Kannengiesser, 11–13 October 2006*, edited by Lorenzo DiTommaso and Lucian Turcescu, 491–510. Bible in Ancient Christianity 6. Leiden: Brill, 2008.

———. *Mary in Early Christian Faith and Devotion*. New Haven: Yale University Press, 2016.

Sim, David C. "Matthew and Ignatius of Antioch." In *Matthew and His Christian Contemporaries*, edited by David C. Sim and Boris Repschinski, 139–54. Library of New Testament Studies 333. London: T. & T. Clark, 2008.

Spain, Suzanne. "The Restoration of the Sta. Maria Maggiore Mosaics." *Art Bulletin* 65 (1983) 325–28.

Stempvoort, P. van. "The Protevangelium Jacobi: The Sources of its Theme and Style and Their Bearing on its Date." In *Studia Evangelica III*, edited by Frank L. Cross, 410–26. TUGAL 88. Berlin: Akademie, 1964.

Stone, Michael E. "The Bones of Adam and Eve." In *For a Later Generation: The Transformation of Tradition in Israel, Early Judaism, and Early Christianity*, edited by Randal A. Argall et al., 241–45. Harrisburg, PA: Trinity, 2000.

Strycker, Émile de. "Die griechischen Handschriften des Protevangeliums Iacobi." In *Griechische Kodikologie und Textüberlieferung*, edited by Dieter Harlfinger, 577–612. Darmstadt: Wissenschaftliche Buchgesellschaft, 1980.

———. "Le Protévangile de Jacques: Problèmes critiques et exégétiques." In *Studia Evangelica III*, edited by Frank L. Cross, 339–59. TUGAL 88. Berlin: Akademie, 1964.

Tyson, Joseph B. *Marcion and Luke-Acts: A Defining Struggle*. Columbia: University of South Carolina Press, 2006.

Vanden Eykel, Eric M. *"But Their Faces Were All Looking Up": Author and Reader in the Protevangelium of James*. Reception of Jesus in the First Three Centuries 1. London: T. & T. Clark, 2016.

Vikan, Gary. *Early Byzantine Pilgrimage Art*. Washington, DC: Dumbarton Oaks Research Library and Collection, 2010.

Vorster, Willem S. "The Annunciation of the Birth of Jesus in the Protevangelium of James." In *A South African Perspective on the New Testament: Esays by South African New Testament Scholars Presented to Bruce Manning Metzger during His Visit to South Africa in 1985*, edited by J. H. Petzer and P. J. Hartin, 33–53. Leiden: Brill, 1986.

———. "The Protevangelium of James and Intertextuality." In *Text and Testimony: Essays on New Testament and Apocryphal Literature in Honour of A. F. J. Klijn*, edited by Tjitze Baarda et al., 265–75. Kampen: Kok, 1988.

Vuong, Lily C. *Gender and Purity in the Protevangelium of James*. WUNT 2/358. Tübingen: Mohr/Siebeck, 2013.

Warland, Rainer. "The Concept of Rome in the Mosaics of the Triumphal Arch of S. Maria Maggiore in Rome." *Acta ad archaeologiam et atrium historiam pertinentia* 17 (2003) 128–29.

Zervos, George T. "Dating the Protevangelium of James: The Justin Martyr Connection." In *Society of Biblical Literature 1994 Seminar Papers*, edited by Eugene H. Lovering, 415–34. SBLSP 33. Atlanta: Scholars, 1994.

—————. "An Early Non-Canonical Annunciation Story." In *Society of Biblical Literature Seminar Papers, 1991*, edited by Eugene H. Lovering, 664–91. SBLSP 30. Atlanta: Scholars, 1997.

—————. "Prolegomena to a Critical Edition of the Genesis Marias (Protevangelium Jacobi): The Greek Manuscripts." PhD diss., Duke University, 1986.

Zetterholm, Magnus. *The Formation of Christianity in Antioch: A Social-Scientific Approach to the Separation between Judaism and Christianity.* New York: Routledge, 2003.

Index of Ancient Sources

m. Sotah

	90
5.1	9

m. Ta'anit

4.8	53

m. Yoma

7.4	52
7.5	58

t. Hullin

2.22–24	27

t. Pesahim

5	17

Classical and Greco-Roman Literature

Achilles Tacitus

Leucippe and Clitophon

	78
5.11.3	29
8.3.3	29
6.1–5	29
13.1—14.2	29

Longus

Daphnis and Chloe

	78
4.28.3	29

New Testament

Matthew

1:1–16	75
1:18	8, 71
1:18–19	73
1:19	8, 86
1:20–23	8
1:20–21	86
1:21	80
1:24	86
1:25	70
2:1–18	10
2:1–7	103
2:8–12	104
2:9	11
2:11	94
2:12	11
2:13–15	11
2:16–18	104
2:19–20	108
3:16	68
4:2	51
10:16	68
11:21	53
12:40	107
13:55–56	73
13:55	13, 19, 28, 71, 92, 108
13:56	91
14:6–11	99
22:12	53
23:35	106
24:14	55
26:13	55
27:4	86
27:28	77
27:42	102
27:45–51	95

Mark

1:9–11	79
1:10	68
3:31–32	70
6:3	19, 28, 70, 73, 91, 92, 108
6:17–28	99
15:17	77